THE OLIVER PROJECT

A Compassionate Guide for a
Final, Loving Goodbye

Angela Human

First Edition

ISBN: 979-8-218-82943-8

Dedicated to our furry mortals who have gone before:

Lucy, Tootie, Liz, Zoey, Zack, and, of course, Oliver

Contents

Contents

Introduction

Furry Mortal (fur·ry mor·tal)

[noun]

A term of endearment used by a devoted parent to refer to any beloved pet, whether the animal is covered in fur, scales, or feathers. The term emphasizes the animal's mortality and vulnerability, underscoring the deep, responsible commitment of the parent to cherish and protect them during their lifespan.

Why This Book?

As someone who has navigated the heartbreaking terrain of pet loss many times and in many ways, I know all too well the weight of end-of-life care and the unique grief that comes with saying goodbye to a beloved pet.

The internet offers a wealth of information yet finding guidance that truly resonates with the depth of our bond with our pets can feel like searching for a single star in a vast night sky. The recent passing of my Bubba (Oliver, as you will know him) served as the poignant reminder that while resources on pet aftercare abound, a comprehensive guide addressing all aspects of end-of-life care (from the initial signs of decline to the final farewell) is desperately needed.

This book is my attempt to illuminate that path, sharing the knowledge I've gained through personal experience and the wisdom so generously offered by others. In these pages, you will find stories of love, loss, and the raw, complex emotions that come with end-of-life care for our beloved companions.

I want to be perfectly clear about the intention of this book: **I am not a veterinarian**, and I do not claim that anything written within these pages constitutes direct medical advice. The stories and insights collected here are born entirely from personal experience. This is a necessary distinction, as the emotional landscape of pet loss is a universal one, regardless of professional background.

This journey with our furry mortals is one of profound love and responsibility. My ultimate goal is to help you navigate it—pet parent to pet parent—providing you with confidence and compassion, so that when the time comes to say goodbye, you can look back on your shared experience with a sense of peace and pride, knowing **you honored your furry mortal with the best possible care until the very end.**

3   Furry Mortals

The Furry Mortal Journey

Oliver

5 Furry Mortals

Oliver - The Spark

"Even when the decision to say goodbye is made with the purest intentions and the pet's best interest at heart. The process itself can leave painful, permanent scars. This is especially true in the moments after a pet has passed. These are the important, tender moments when compassion and understanding are paramount; yet, as I tragically discovered, they can sometimes be profoundly absent.

This is the story of Oliver, my Bubba, and the unexpected kick in the gut that compelled me to write this book. He was truly "the one who inspired this book." And he was truly my "that one".

I want you to know Oliver. He was a magnificent, big teddy bear, a furry embodiment of love, kisses, and endless smiles. He personified pure love and happiness in one giant, lovable package.

Oliver (Bandit then) came from Blue Heron Farm. They were fostering him, he was their second foster, Charlotte, his sister, was their first and she had been adopted. We went out for a "meet & greet" with Zack (our border collie) to see if Oliver would be a good fit. We walked into their front yard, I saw them open the front door and I got down low and here comes Oliver, bounding out that door and into my arms almost knocking me over. And with that, Laurel knew at that moment this was no longer a "meet & greet".

They sent us home with a dog and roll of blue shop towels because they did not know if he got sick riding in the car (he did not). He had only been at his foster for one day, he had been feral for 6 months, so he came with very few manners which was unlike our VERY well-mannered Zack. But Oliver was a fast learner … so super smart. Lisa and Christian said he would be about 35 lbs. full grown. Well … when he started getting good food, Bubba kept growing and growing topping at 80 lbs. They have apologized many times since, but we loved him exactly the way he was.

Everyone LOVED Oliver. And he gave everyone love in return despite his very scary appearance. He had big bear paw feet, and that big head and booming bark could scare off anyone. He never saw a meal he didn't love and LOVED to wear clothes. He had a complete wardrobe of T-shirts, pjs, sweatshirts, sweaters, jackets and vests. His dapper brother also had a wardrobe, but it was much more preppy. To say he and Zack were the best of friends would be an understatement. They were inseparable.

One day we noticed Oliver starting to really slow down, his breathing was becoming heavier, and his walking grew more labored. We were diligently managing his hip dysplasia, a condition we knew well. But it was the labored breathing that heralded his final goodbye.

Following our vet's suggestion, we took Bubba to the emergency clinic. The X-rays revealed a devastating truth: cancer had spread aggressively to his lungs, so much so that the veterinarians were astonished he was even breathing on his own. This news hit me like a physical blow. How could this have been missed? How could such a virulent disease have spread without any prior indication (at least no indication to me)? The shock was immense, and we were faced with the agonizing decision to say goodbye right then. He was suffering, and though he would undoubtedly keep fighting for us, we couldn't ask him to endure any more.

The veterinarian on call and the initial vet tech were truly fabulous, guiding us through those first, devastating moments with kindness and professionalism and even shared sadness. But things took a drastic turn for the worse after Bubba had passed. After we had taken a moment to love on him, even after he was gone, we signaled we were ready to leave. Another vet tech entered the room. She didn't know Bubba's name or ours, simply pointed to a door, and said "That will take you out." Then, without a word, she proceeded to pull out the oxygen hoses and IVs from Bubba's body before we could even exit the room. Stunned, I managed to ask what was next, and her response was curt: "IT will be taken care of, and we will let you know when IT is ready." I was utterly shattered, grieving so intensely that all I could do was leave.

The trauma didn't end there. When we returned to the same clinic to pick up Bubba's urn, I was made to wait in the overly busy lobby at the check-in counter, exposed and vulnerable. The woman who brought out his urn, inexplicably, had a bad, laughing demeanor and exclaimed, "Wow, he was a big boy!" I was once again in shock, crying too hard to explain to her that this was all wrong, that her casual comment was an additional, agonizing blow. It was in the raw aftermath of Oliver's goodbye that a fierce determination ignited within me.

This experience solidified my resolve to write this book. The profound lack of empathy and respect after Bubba's passing, and the handling of his remains, was something I couldn't ignore. This is for Bubba, for all pet parents navigating this journey, and for the clinic staff who have the power to make these final moments, and their aftermath, truly compassionate.

We must do better."

— Angela, Bubba's Mom

"Being Mortal" for Furry Mortals

It all started on a long plane ride during a family vacation to Italy. My nephew, who was gearing up for medical school, handed me his copy of a book called *Being Mortal* "Everyone, especially doctors, should read this," he told me. I dove in, and it quickly became one of the most significant books I would ever read.

As someone already working in the world of human end-of-life care, the concepts immediately clicked with me. I understood the difficult choices, the dilemmas, and the heartbreaking reality human families face. But honestly, the truly profound impact—the big, undeniable lightbulb moment—didn't hit me until much later, after I went through the tragic loss of my own beloved Bubba, Oliver.

When Oliver passed, I was completely shattered by how little dignity and compassion there was in his final moments. And that's when the ideas from *Being Mortal* rushed back to me with new, urgent meaning. I realized that the same painful, difficult choices people face at the end of their lives—like choosing comfort and dignity over simply extending time—are the exact choices we, as pet parents, struggle with, too. It was a powerful realization: the principles for a good, dignified goodbye for a person should absolutely apply to our beloved furry mortals.

Fast-forward a few years: my nephew is now a doctor, and I'm writing this book based on that very idea. The difference, of course, is that my focus is on end-of-life care for our pets.

Atul Gawande's insightful book highlights how focusing purely on medical treatment often completely misses the human experience of dying. He, as a practicing surgeon, noticed early in his training the huge emphasis on treating disease and prolonging life, often at the expense of addressing mortality itself.

That same gap exists in veterinary medicine. We have incredible medical advancements to treat diseases and prolong a pet's lifespan. But sometimes, that intense focus on fighting disease can overshadow what's truly important in our pet's final chapter: their comfort and overall quality of life. *Being Mortal* centers on this fundamental conflict: the drive to prolong life versus the vital necessity of ensuring a meaningful quality of life. This principle, of balancing longevity with quality of life, is just as relevant for our animal companions. We need to recognize that mere survival shouldn't come at the cost of our pet's comfort, dignity, or ability to experience joy.

Gawande powerfully advocates for having open and honest conversations about death and dying. He shows that when we sidestep these challenging discussions, we leave people—and their families—unprepared for the realities of mortality, which can result in needless suffering.

Similarly, I know that as pet parents, we often have a tendency to completely avoid thinking or talking about the end of our pet's life. Fostering open communication with our vets about the possibilities and realities of a pet's declining health is absolutely essential. It's how *we* can make it ok to have these discussions and make sure our decisions are made with compassion and foresight.

Historically, many pets simply died at home with minimal intervention. But with veterinary medicine advancing, we've seen a parallel rise in more clinical approaches to pet aging and death. While this has led to wonderful, specialized options like pet hospice and comfort care, the limitations of relying *only* on this approach can inadvertently lead to increased suffering and a diminished quality of life for both pets and their parents. When the goal is just to fight the disease and prolong life at *any* cost, we can easily overlook our pet's emotional, environmental, and overall well-being. **This is why an integrated holistic approach is so important.**

A holistic approach goes beyond just addressing physical ailments. It takes into account the interconnectedness of our pet's physical comfort, emotional well-being, and the environment they live in. Each animal is unique—they have a unique personality, unique needs, and their own way of experiencing the world. I believe a truly compassionate approach *must* consider these individual factors when making decisions about their care in their final stages.

The fact is, our pets are cherished family members now more than ever. This deep bond is fueling a growing demand for care options that prioritize their comfort, emotional well-being, and overall quality of life, mirroring the principles of the human hospice movement.

By drawing parallels with the deep insights I found in *Being Mortal*, Furry Mortals aims to empower *you* to make informed decisions that prioritize your pet's comfort, dignity, and the precious bond you share. I want to give you practical strategies and compassionate guidance for navigating this challenging journey, ensuring your pet's final days are as comfortable and meaningful as possible.

A quick note from me: I am largely exploring pet parenting and end-of-life care through a Western cultural lens. I encourage you to remember and respect that beliefs and practices around pet end-of-life care can vary significantly across different cultures and traditions.

The Path to Now

Historically, the passing of a pet often occurred naturally without extensive medical intervention, but modern veterinary medicine has significantly changed this reality. Thanks to advancements in nutrition, preventative care, and treatment, our pets are living longer and, as a result, are more likely to experience age-related and chronic illnesses. This longevity offers us more time with our companions but also presents new challenges for end-of-life care.

The sophisticated nature of modern veterinary medicine, while a phenomenal benefit, has introduced a heavy paradox into the final phase of pet parenthood. **We now grapple with a wider array of choices and challenges, often under considerable emotional strain.** No longer is the path clearly defined by nature. Instead, pet parents must navigate a complex landscape of medical possibilities, each carrying its own emotional and financial weight.

We face the choice between pursuing aggressive, life-extending treatments (like surgery, chemotherapy, or continuous specialized care) versus opting for palliative comfort care. This requires weighing the potential gain in time against the guaranteed loss of quality of life, the financial cost, and the emotional burden on the pet. We, as pet parents, must ask ourselves if we should fight for two more months of difficult treatment, or ensure two weeks of joyful, comfortable living.

With pets living longer, we often become primary caregivers for chronic conditions like severe arthritis, diabetes, kidney failure, or cognitive dysfunction. This involves a daily routine of medication, injections, dietary management, and symptom monitoring. The sheer volume of this work—the constant vigilance and practical tasks—is the core of caregiver burden.

The increasing use of pet hospice and comfort care programs represents a positive societal shift. This trend moves away from a singular focus on extending life and toward a more comprehensive, compassionate approach that prioritizes our pets' comfort, dignity, and overall well-being as they approach the end of their lives. This approach allows us to make choices that align with our values and our pet's best interests, ensuring a peaceful and humane farewell.

But, perhaps the most profound challenge is the agonizing, solitary decision regarding euthanasia. In the past, nature often decided. Now, the final decision rests squarely with us. This responsibility is compounded by the knowledge that we *could* potentially extend life, leading to profound **guilt, self-doubt, and the fear of deciding too soon or too late**. We struggle to reconcile our deep desire to keep them with us with the ethical imperative to relieve their suffering.

Advanced care can be incredibly expensive. Pet parents must contend not just with grief, but with the practical stress of balancing their own family's financial security against their pet's care needs. This can lead to a moral strain where love conflicts with resources, fueling feelings of shame or inadequacy.

While we are better equipped medically, the deep emotional processing remains intensely personal. The significant emotional strain often comes from a lack of societal understanding—friends or employers may not recognize the intensity of grief over a pet, leading to a sense of isolation when support is needed most.

We must also think of the veterinary professionals and the challenges they face. Time constraints in busy practices can make it difficult for them to provide the necessary time for in-depth discussions and emotional support. They can also experience emotional fatigue and burnout from repeatedly supporting us through this difficult time.

The totality of these choices: medical, financial, and emotional, creates an intense period of stress, making the pet's end-of-life journey a profound test of endurance and love.

This landscape of modern options highlights why a shift toward a holistic perspective is not just a luxury, but a necessity. When we move away from a purely medicalized view of death, we begin to see that "care" isn't always synonymous with "cure." It allows us to view the end of life as a sacred season of transition rather than a battle to be won or lost.

By integrating the physical, emotional, and environmental elements of our pets' lives, we can transform a period characterized by anxiety and medical treatments into one of deep connection and presence. This holistic lens helps us filter through the noise of endless medical choices to find the path that honors the specific, unique soul of our "furry mortal," ensuring that their final chapter is written with the same love and intention as their first.

Comfort Beyond Medicine

First, I want to dispel the myth that adopting a holistic approach to end-of-life care for your pet means a complete departure from conventional veterinary medicine. In fact, the most effective and compassionate approach is often a combination of both. Conventional medicine provides important tools like diagnostic testing, pain medication, and comfort treatments for symptom management. A holistic approach then complements these therapies with a focus on the pet's overall well-being, incorporating methods like acupuncture for pain relief, nutritional adjustments to support organ function, or herbal supplements to manage anxiety. By integrating the best of both worlds, you can provide your pet with comprehensive care that not only addresses the physical symptoms of their illness but also nurtures their emotional and mental comfort, ensuring their final days are as peaceful and dignified as possible. **All of our pets have had a combination of both holistic and conventional treatments, at their end-of-life.**

Holistic healthcare for pets at the end of life is grounded in the core principles of interconnectedness, individualized care, and addressing the underlying factors that contribute to well-being. This approach moves beyond simply treating the symptoms of illness and instead **considers the whole pet – their physical body, their emotional state, and their interaction with their environment**. Recognizing that each animal is unique, holistic care emphasizes tailoring care plans to meet the specific needs and preferences of every individual pet.

The key components of holistic end-of-life care for pets can be broadly categorized into physical comfort, emotional well-being, and environmental comfort. Physical comfort focuses on managing pain effectively through various methods, including medications and complementary therapies. It also involves providing support for mobility issues through aids like slings or ramps, ensuring proper hygiene to prevent discomfort and infection, and addressing nutritional and hydration needs to maintain strength and organ function.

Emotional well-being is another critical aspect of holistic care. This involves creating a calm and supportive environment to reduce stress and anxiety in a pet's final days. Maintaining a sense of security and connection through gentle interaction and the presence of familiar caregivers is paramount. Addressing any behavioral changes that may arise due to illness or cognitive decline is also an important part of supporting a pet's emotional comfort.

Environmental comfort focuses on adapting the pet's living space to meet their changing needs. This includes creating a safe and easily accessible environment, providing comfortable bedding, and ensuring that food, water, and elimination areas are within easy reach. Minimizing stressors in the environment, such as loud noises or disruptions, can also contribute to a pet's peace and comfort.

All these components are of vital importance to our human-animal bond. This bond provides a source of comfort, security, and meaning for both the pet and the caregiver during the end-of-life journey. Nurturing this connection through gentle touch, quiet companionship, and simply being present with our pet is the cornerstone of holistic care.

Holistic end-of-life care for pets recognizes the intricate connections between a pet's physical state, their emotional well-being, and the environment in which they live. Addressing pain alone is not sufficient; a truly holistic approach considers the pet's emotional state, their comfort within their surroundings, and the strength of their bond with their human family. A pet's emotional state can directly influence their physical health, and conversely, physical discomfort can significantly impact their emotional well-being. For instance, pain can lead to increased anxiety and depression, while a stressful environment can exacerbate physical symptoms.

When you focus on nurturing that love, you're not just giving your pet comfort and security; you're also giving yourself a vital sense of purpose. It's the powerful connection between you two that makes this challenging end-of-life journey manageable and allows for a truly meaningful goodbye.

In my experience, the deep bond we share with our pets is the greatest source of strength during this painful chapter. **It's what anchors us.**

Grasping Their Reality

It is essential to discuss the core of a compassionate approach to the end of our pet's life—**shifting focus from simply extending life to profoundly enriching the time remaining**. To truly honor the unique journey of a beloved animal, we must move beyond the clinical chart and embrace the art of observation.

When facing the impending loss of a beloved pet, our natural inclination is to focus on the medical. We pore over diagnoses, track symptoms, and diligently administer medications, all in an effort to extend their time or alleviate their pain. This is vital, of course. Yet, with all the clinical considerations, it's easy to overlook what our pets are truly feeling inside as they decline. Just as we strive to understand and honor human mortality, so too must we endeavor to grasp what it means for our animal companions to approach the end of their lives.

Inspired by profound discussions of human mortality, we can begin to appreciate that our pets, too, have a "world" that undergoes significant transformation as they near their final days. Their existence, once vibrant and predictable, begins to narrow. Activities they once relished may become arduous or unappealing. Their perception of their own body might shift, bringing discomfort or weakness. Understanding these changes, even if we can only infer them, is the first step toward providing a truly compassionate farewell.

When decline begins, we must remember, our pets don't speak our language, but they communicate volumes through their behavior. As their bodies begin to fail, even subtly, you'll likely observe shifts in their daily routines and interactions. These aren't always overt signs of pain; sometimes, they are more nuanced expressions of their changing reality.

For instance, a once-enthusiastic dog might show less interest in walks, preferring a shorter stroll or even just a putter in the yard. A cat who once greeted you at the door might now remain curled up in their favorite spot. Appetite changes are common, ranging from pickiness to complete disinterest in food. You might notice changes in their sleep patterns—more frequent napping, or restlessness at night.

Beyond physical manifestations, pay close attention to behavioral shifts that indicate emotional responses. Anxious pets might become clingier, seeking constant reassurance, or conversely, they might withdraw and seek solitude. Increased vocalization, pacing, or aimless wandering could signal confusion or discomfort. Conversely, a pet who was once independent might suddenly crave more physical closeness, leaning into your touch or sleeping closer to you than usual. These are their ways of telling you that their world is changing, and they need your comfort and understanding more than ever.

For animals, routine provides a profound sense of security and predictability. As they decline, maintaining familiar routines, even in modified forms, can be incredibly grounding. If walks become too much, perhaps a gentle car ride is still enjoyable. If their favorite playtime is too strenuous, a quiet cuddle session can offer immense comfort. Disrupting their established rhythms unnecessarily can add to their stress and confusion.

Equally important is their environment. As their mobility or senses diminish, their surroundings might feel overwhelming or unsafe. Ensure their resting places are easily accessible, soft, and warm. Minimize loud noises or sudden movements that could startle them. Consider their eyesight and hearing; a brightly lit room might be disorienting for a pet with failing vision, while a quiet space might be more comforting for one with sensitive hearing. The goal is to create a sanctuary where they feel safe, secure, and at peace.

And then there are the social bonds, the bedrock of their existence. Your presence, your touch, your voice are powerful anchors in their diminishing world. Continue to engage with them, even if it's just through quiet petting or gentle conversation. **Let them know they are loved, seen, and not alone.** Their need for connection often intensifies, and providing that constant, reassuring presence can alleviate anxiety and fear. It's not about forcing interactions, but rather being available and responsive to their cues, honoring their need for companionship on their own terms.

The core of compassionate pet end-of-life care lies in shifting our focus from **solely extending life** to **profoundly enriching the time remaining** by observing and honoring their non-verbal cues and providing security through modified routines and a comforting environment.

A "Good Death" from Their Perspective

What truly constitutes a "good death" for a pet? It's a question that challenges us to look beyond a purely clinical prognosis and instead value their subjective experience. This is the core principle of Atul Gawande's guidance in *Being Mortal*, which teaches us that a good life isn't just about survival, but about well-being. Applying this to our animal companions, a good death isn't merely the absence of pain, though that is paramount. It's about preserving their dignity and their sense of self for as long as possible.

A good death is about ensuring your pet's final days are lived with a continued sense of security, peace, and love, rather than being solely defined by medical management. It's a profound shift in perspective, moving from what we can *do for them* medically to what we can *do for them* emotionally and existentially.

A good death starts with dignity. For a pet, dignity is the ability to still be themselves, even when their body is failing. It's the ability for a dog to still sniff the grass on a short, slow walk, or for a cat to still choose their favorite sunbeam for a nap. It means keeping them as clean and comfortable as possible, addressing incontinence without shame, and maintaining their routines as best you can. When a pet can no longer move on their own, dignity is in the soft blanket, the gentle repositioning, and the human presence that reassures them they are safe and loved.

As a pet's health declines, the conversation often shifts from curative treatments to managing symptoms. This is where prioritizing quality of life over quantity becomes essential. An aggressive treatment that requires frequent, stressful vet visits, painful procedures, or causes debilitating side effects may extend their life by a few weeks or months, but at what cost? A good death may mean making the difficult choice to decline a procedure and instead focus on providing a peaceful environment at home, filled with their favorite blankets, gentle words, and familiar scents. It is a decision that honors their well-being in the present moment, rather than clinging to a future that may hold more suffering.

Our pets communicate with us in a language of subtle cues. As their caregiver, you are uniquely positioned to interpret these signs. A dog's lowered head, a cat's refusal to purr, a lack of interest in a favorite treat, these are not just signs of illness. They are expressions of your pet's subjective experience. They tell you about their joy, their discomfort, and their desire for peace. By becoming a close observer of these cues, you can more accurately gauge when their joy is outweighed by their suffering, helping you to make compassionate decisions that are truly in their best interest.

A good death often culminates in the most difficult decision of all: euthanasia. It is important to reframe this decision not as "giving up," but as the final, most selfless act of love. When you make this choice, you are taking on your pet's pain and sadness so that they don't have to endure it. A peaceful euthanasia, performed in a familiar, calm environment with family present, allows a pet to transition with dignity, free from distress, and surrounded by the love that defined their life.

A "good death" is not defined by the date on a calendar or the specifics of a medical chart, but by the quiet grace of a life held in transition. It is the final stewardship of a soul that has given you its entire world without reservation. By choosing to prioritize their peace over our desire for more time, we transform our grief into a sanctuary for them. In those final moments, when the clinical noise fades and only the rhythm of a familiar breath remains, the greatest gift we can offer is the assurance that they are not a patient to be managed, but a beloved family member being walked home.

Hopefully this book inspires you to look beyond the illness and connect with your pet's emotional and existential journey. By interpreting their subtle cues, honoring their routines, creating a comforting environment, and cherishing your bond, you can ensure their final chapter is imbued with dignity, love, and a profound sense of peace. **It's a testament to the enduring power of the human-animal bond, guiding them gently through their last moments and allowing them to depart with grace.**

furry mortal

[noun]

A temporary guardian of our joy who loves without reservation, ages with dignity, and eventually leaves a paw-shaped void that only a lifetime of memories can fill

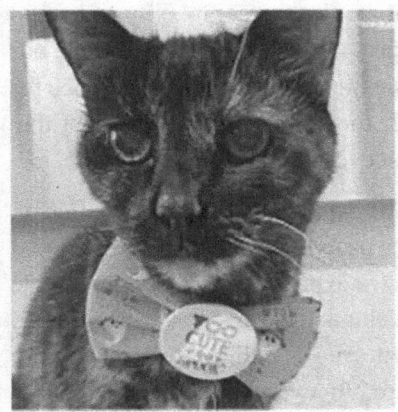

Reflection 1

A Debt of Unconditional Love

The moment a pair of tiny paws first skids across a hardwood floor or a soft, rhythmic purr vibrates against a new blanket, a clock begins to tick. It is a silent, internal countdown that we, in our initial ecstasy, choose to ignore. We are too busy laughing at the bounding chaos, the alert ears, and the wagging tails that have effectively dismantled the quiet of our former lives. In that threshold moment, a contract is signed—not in ink, but in a promise that settles deep within the marrow of the soul. It is a bargain of absolute loyalty and a treasure trove of secrets that only our furry mortals are capable of keeping.

As the days turn into seasons, we begin to measure our lives through a new and beautiful lens. We stop counting minutes and start counting the "happy, easy sighs" exhaled at the foot of our beds. We find our rhythm in the cold, wet-nosed nudges that demand our presence before the sun has fully crested the horizon. We live under the honest, unwavering gaze of eyes that do not require the complexity of human language to tell us exactly who we are. In this exchange, we trade our finite time for a single sloppy kiss; we trade our dwindling patience for the sight of a shredded toy. It feels, for a long time, like a debt that costs us nothing but provides us with everything.

However, the premise of this book—and the reality of being an advocate for a furry mortal—requires us to look at the fine print of that initial contract. Every singular bliss we experience is a payment made in advance. Every gentle scratch behind the ears and every heavy, warm nap stretched out on a favorite rug is a line of credit we are drawing against the future. We are, in every sense, taking out a "mortgage of the heart." We are accumulating a tally of joy that we must one day reconcile, and the currency of that final payment is a sorrow as definitive as the love that preceded it.

The tragedy of the human-animal bond is that the story is written before the first chapter even ends. The bargain is struck the moment we decide to love a creature whose internal clock runs so much faster than our own. The very reason our hearts soar when they greet us at the door is the same reason those hearts will eventually break. We are signing up for the "final, broken heart" from the very first day. This isn't a failure of the system; it is the system itself. It is the cost of admission for the privilege of being known and loved by a heart that knows no guile, no hidden agenda, and no conditions.

As we navigate the end-of-life journey, we must realize that our grief is not a debt that has gone into default. Rather, it is the full payment of the mortgage we took out a decade or more ago. Being a fierce advocate for your pet is accepting this broken heart as a badge of honor. It is proof that the treasure was real. When we stand in that final, quiet room, or sit together under a favorite tree for the last time, we aren't just losing a friend; we are fulfilling our end of the most honest contract we will ever sign.

We are paying the price of unconditional love, and in the end, we find that the treasure was worth every bit of the sorrow we must now carry.

Enhancing Quality of Life

29 Furry Mortals

BG - The Legacy of Past Generations

"BG was my "first" dog, my childhood dog. When I was little she was my very best friend. We spent hours and hours together in the backyard doing anything and everything. I was an only child, so she filled that spot of a "sibling" for me. She was my confidant, my shoulder to lean on and a soft pillow to lay on and read and look at the clouds. She did not care if I had cut my own bangs or was the biggest nerd out there. She loved me unconditionally and I her.

My parents, belonging to the "Baby Boomer" generation, held a significantly different outlook on pet care than is common today. When BG was diagnosed with breast cancer, their approach reflected this generational difference. My dad, driven by a belief that surgical treatment would only cause her cancer to spread faster, made the difficult decision to forego veterinary intervention. He brought BG home, committed to keeping her comfortable and safe under his own roof. This choice was born from a deep-seated need to protect her from what he perceived as unnecessary risk.

My dad also harbored a profound, heart-wrenching fear: that if he took BG back to the veterinarian for euthanasia, they would not return her body to him. This fear, while contrary to standard practice, wasn't a sign of mistrust; it was a profound testament to the overwhelming, all-consuming love he felt for his dog and the emotional weight of planning her final goodbye without the compassionate, educational support that is common today.

My dad's actions were driven solely and completely by love. BG was his best friend, his steadfast companion. He sat by her side, comforting her until she crossed the rainbow bridge at home. The loss of BG devastated him so deeply that he vowed never to have another dog, believing the pain of a second goodbye would be unbearable. Though his approach to her end-of-life care was undeniably clouded by the lack of educational resources and understanding available in that era, it was his extraordinary love for her that served as his ultimate, though imperfect, guide. BG rests now, in a place of honor, buried under a beautiful lilac tree at my childhood home, exactly where my dad tenderly placed her.

BG's story, while painful for me to tell, beautifully illustrates the depth of a father's love and the complexity of end-of-life choices made without modern understanding."
— **Angela, BG's Little Best Friend**

The Approaching End

Recognizing when our beloved pet is nearing the end of their life is a deeply emotional and often challenging process. However, being attuned to the subtle and overt signs of declining health can help us provide the most appropriate care and make timely decisions. These indicators often manifest as gradual shifts in our pet's daily routines and overall well-being.

Changes in our pet's appetite and water intake are often among the first noticeable signs. Our pet may eat less, become finicky about their food, or even stop eating altogether. Their drinking habits might change, with some drinking significantly more or less than usual. Lethargy and decreased activity levels are also common indicators. A pet that once enjoyed walks or playtime may become increasingly tired, sleep more, and show less enthusiasm for their usual activities.

Changes in sleep patterns can also signal declining health. Our pet might sleep more during the day and be restless at night, or their usual sleeping habits may simply become erratic. A loss of interest in favorite activities and social interaction is another key sign. A dog that once greeted us enthusiastically at the door might become withdrawn, or a cat that enjoyed cuddling might seek solitude.

Difficulties with mobility and coordination are often apparent as our pet ages or becomes ill. This can manifest as stiffness, reluctance to jump or climb stairs, stumbling, or a general decrease in their ability to move around comfortably. Changes in elimination habits can also indicate a decline in health. This might include increased frequency of urination or defecation, accidents inside the house, or difficulty controlling their bladder or bowels.

Signs of pain or discomfort can be subtle but are important for us to recognize. I have seen these signs as excessive panting, restlessness, vocalization, reluctance to be touched, or changes in posture. Finally, changes in our pet's demeanor and behavior can be significant indicators. A once friendly pet might become irritable, or a usually confident animal might appear anxious or confused.

The signs that our pet is approaching the end of their life often manifest as a gradual decline across multiple areas of their well-being, rather than a sudden, dramatic event. We should pay close attention to even subtle shifts in our pet's daily routines and behaviors, as these can be early indicators of declining health and the need to consider end-of-life care options. Pain and discomfort can significantly impact our pet's overall quality of life, leading to decreased engagement and enjoyment of their usual activities.

Recognizing and effectively managing any signs of pain is paramount in providing comfort and maintaining a reasonable quality of life for our pet nearing the end of their journey. Early recognition of these indicators allows us to proactively engage in discussions with our veterinarians about end-of-life care, leading to a more prepared and less reactive approach. This proactive stance can result in better planning, reducing stress, and more informed decision-making that prioritizes our pet's best interests. It is vital for us to maintain close observation of our pets and communicate any concerns or changes in behavior to our veterinarian.

The challenging process of recognizing our pet's declining health requires us to be fully aware of the subtle changes in appetite, activity, mobility, pain indicators, and behavior. This in turn enables us to proactively plan and execute compassionate end-of-life care.

Beyond the clinical checklists and physical markers lies the quiet intuition of the bond you share. As a caregiver, you possess a unique literacy in your pet's soul that no medical test can replicate. There often comes a moment when the light in their eyes changes, or a specific stillness settles over them, signaling that they are ready to let go.

Honoring this intuitive nudge is just as vital as monitoring their mobility or appetite. It is the final conversation in a lifelong dialogue of trust, reminding us that while the mind seeks data to justify a decision, the heart often already knows the way. **Embracing this internal compass allows us to transition from a place of frantic caretaking to one of peaceful accompaniment.**

Your Veterinarian as a Partner

Veterinarians play an important role in guiding and supporting pet parents through the often-uncharted territory of end-of-life care. Their expertise extends beyond medical knowledge to encompass compassionate communication, ethical considerations, and a commitment to the well-being of both the pet and their human family. A non-negotiable aspect of this partnership involves facilitating open and honest conversations about the pet's prognosis, the available care options, and the potential outcomes.

When a diagnosis of terminal illness takes place, we are often in shock. We are not thinking clearly when we hear the words "cancer" or "congestive heart failure" so we often do not hear or think of anything after those words are uttered. But at this stage, open communication is vital for the care of our pets. We must ask the important questions even if we are too scared to hear the answers, like:

- "What is the typical progression of this illness?"
- "What are the signs of pain versus non-painful symptoms?"
- "What are the goals of comfort care vs. curative treatment for this condition?"
- "If we choose not to pursue treatment, what will the end look like?"

Veterinarians play a key role in developing individualized comfort and hospice care plans tailored to the specific needs and circumstances of each pet and their parent. This includes recommending appropriate pain management strategies, which may involve a combination of pharmaceutical medications and complementary therapies.

They also guide parents on managing other distressing symptoms and provide emotional support throughout the process. When the time comes, veterinarians play a vital role in performing humane euthanasia with compassion and dignity.

Ethical considerations are paramount in end-of-life care. **Vets are guided by two main ideas: always doing what's best for the pet and making sure they don't cause any harm.** This means prioritizing the pet's well-being and avoiding unnecessary or overly aggressive interventions that may prolong suffering without improving quality of life. Balancing the pet's needs with the parent's capabilities, values, and financial constraints is also an important ethical consideration.

A collaborative partnership between the pet parent and the veterinary team is essential for providing the best possible end-of-life care. This involves open communication, shared decision-making, and a mutual commitment to ensuring the pet's comfort and dignity in their final moments.

The evolving field of veterinary medicine increasingly recognizes end-of-life care as a critical component of comprehensive animal care, requiring specialized knowledge, skills, and a deep sense of empathy.

Measuring Quality of Life

When faced with the end of a pet's life, the most compassionate approach is to look beyond a purely clinical prognosis and instead value how your pet actually feels. This is the core principle of Atul Gawande's *Being Mortal* applied to our animal companions. Simply measuring how long an animal lives is often less meaningful than evaluating the quality of that remaining time. Quality of life (QOL) assessment provides a practical framework for this shift, empowering you as a pet parent and your veterinarian to objectively evaluate your pet's current state and make informed decisions about their care, ensuring their final days are filled with comfort, dignity, and a sense of well-being.

Several QOL assessment tools and scales have been developed specifically for pets, offering guidance on the factors to consider. One widely recognized tool is the *HHHHHMM* scale. This acronym stands for Hurt (adequate pain control), Hunger (eating enough), Hydration (proper fluid intake), Hygiene (cleanliness), Happiness (joy and interest), Mobility (ability to move), and more good days than bad. Pet parents are asked to score their pet in each of these categories, providing a numerical representation of their overall well-being.

Another valuable tool is the *JOURNEYS* scale. This scale considers Jumping/Mobility, Ouch/Pain, Uncertainty/Understanding (related to the caregiver's ability to manage the pet's condition), Respiration/Breathing, Neatness/Hygiene, Eating/Drinking, You (the caregiver's well-being), and social ability. Like the HHHHHMM scale, pet parents assign a score to each category based on their observations.

Other available resources include the *Lap of Love's QOL* scale and the Ohio State University's QOL assessment. These tools often use a questionnaire format, prompting pet parents to reflect on various aspects of their pet's daily life and behaviors to gain a better understanding of their overall well-being.

I created The Furry Mortals QOL Assessment Tool (included in the back of the book) to give pet parents a single, comprehensive tool that **simplifies the difficult process of evaluating their pet's quality of life**. Combining the strengths of established scales into a single, user-friendly resource, it pulls key metrics from tools like the *HHHHHMM Scale* (Hurt, Hunger, Hydration, Hygiene, Happiness, Mobility, More good days than bad) and the *JOURNEYS Scale* (Jumping/Mobility, Ouch/Pain, Uncertainty, Respiration, Neatness, Eating/Drinking, You, Social ability). By doing so, this tool offers a comprehensive framework that goes beyond just the physical symptoms, also considering a pet's emotional well-being, social interaction, and even the caregiver's own capacity to provide care. **This combined approach makes it easier for you to track your pet's journey and have objective, informed conversations with your veterinarian about end-of-life care.**

Using a QOL assessment tool can help you approach the evaluation of your pet's condition in a more structured and objective manner. By regularly monitoring and scoring your pet across different categories, you can track changes over time and identify potential areas of concern. However, it is also important to remember that QOL is inherently subjective. What constitutes a good quality of life for one pet may differ for another based on their individual personality, breed characteristics, and lifelong preferences. For instance, a less active senior dog might still have a good quality of life if they are comfortable and enjoy their quiet routines, while a normally energetic breed might show a significant decline in QOL with even minor limitations.

Your end-of-life care specialist plays a vital role in guiding you through the process of QOL assessment and helping you interpret the results. They can provide valuable insights based on their medical knowledge and observations during examinations, helping you differentiate between normal age-related changes and signs of significant decline. The collaborative use of QOL assessments can facilitate open communication between you and your veterinarian, ensuring that end-of-life decisions are made with a comprehensive understanding of your pet's overall well-being and in their best interest.

Quality of life assessment is not a static measure but a dynamic and ongoing process that requires regular evaluation. It involves continuously monitoring your pet's ability to participate in activities they once enjoyed, their levels of comfort, and their overall happiness. Utilizing a QOL scale can provide you with a more objective perspective on your pet's condition, potentially mitigating emotional biases that can sometimes cloud your judgment. By systematically evaluating different aspects of your pet's life, you can gain a clearer understanding of when the bad days might be outweighing the good. This shift reflects a more ethical and compassionate approach to care, ensuring that you make decisions in your pet's best interest, considering their overall well-being rather than solely focusing on prolonging life.

The most compassionate approach to our pet's end-of-life care must move beyond a clinical prognosis to prioritize the pet's experience. By utilizing Quality of Life (QOL) assessment scales to evaluate their comfort, dignity, and well-being, we empower ourselves to make informed decisions.

The Furry Mortal QOL Assessment Tool

Prioritizing Dignity and Peace

Our journey as pet parents is profoundly defined by our desire to provide a life filled with comfort, joy, and unconditional love. As our pet nears the end of its life, this desire intensifies, shifting our focus to ensuring a peaceful and dignified farewell. When we face the decline of our Furry Mortal, the sheer act of evaluating their quality of life can feel paralyzing. We are often presented with excellent, yet complex, professional frameworks designed to bring objectivity to this highly emotional process.

Attempting to navigate multiple checklists during a crisis can add unnecessary anxiety to an already unbearable time. This is precisely why the Furry Mortals QOL Assessment Tool was created: to consolidate the strengths of these established scales into a single, comprehensive, and cohesive resource. Our tool transforms the best metrics from these frameworks into a unified system that turns your intuitive observations into clear, actionable data.

By prioritizing dignity and peace through this consolidated framework, we can move beyond emotional turmoil to make informed decisions we can feel at peace with, knowing we have honored our pet's best interests and cherished bond.

The Three Pillars of a Holistic Farewell

A truly compassionate approach to end-of-life care for our pets recognizes the interconnectedness of their physical, emotional, and environmental states. Our pet's quality of life isn't a single, isolated variable; it's a dynamic system influenced by numerous factors. To provide a comprehensive framework for evaluation, our assessment tool is structured around three key pillars: **Physical Well-being, Emotional Well-being, and Environmental & Caregiver Well-being**. This integrated model moves beyond a singular focus on disease and instead considers our whole animal and its relationship with our human family.

The first pillar, **Physical Well-being**, addresses the most direct and observable aspects of your pet's health, such as pain management, mobility, and core bodily functions. While essential, this pillar alone is insufficient. Your pet's quality of life can diminish significantly even when physical ailments are managed, as evidenced by stories of pets who withdraw socially or lose their sense of joy.

This is where the second pillar, **Emotional Well-being**, becomes imperative. This pillar focuses on your pet's mental state, happiness, and social connection. It acknowledges that your pet's emotional and psychological suffering is as valid as its physical pain. For instance, chronic pain can lead to emotional withdrawal and anxiety, while a loving and supportive environment can help our pet cope with physical limitations. Our assessment tool gives equal weight to these non-physical indicators, ensuring that your pet's subjective experience is fully considered.

The third and final pillar, **Environmental & Caregiver Well-being**, expands the scope of our quality-of-life assessment to include your pet's living space and your family's capacity to provide care. This pillar recognizes that the human-animal bond is a central component of end-of-life care. Your pet's comfort is directly impacted by its environment, and our family's well-being can be significantly affected by the emotional, physical, and financial toll of caregiving. By including metrics on home modifications, caregiver stress, and proactive planning, our assessment tool formalizes the understanding that **the quality of life for our furry mortals and our family are inextricably linked**.

The "Joy List"

We spend so much of our time as caregivers focused on the "must-dos"—the pill schedules, the mobility harnesses, and the clinical monitoring of breaths per minute. It's easy to let the heavy cloud of "the end" overshadow the vibrant life that is still right in front of us.

While we cannot control the quantity of days remaining, we have absolute agency over their quality. This is where the **Joy List** (or what some call a "Bucket List") comes in. It is a transition from clinical care to pure, unadulterated connection. It is about making sure that your pet's final chapter isn't just about a diagnosis, but about the things that made their tail wag in the first place.

Permission to Indulge

For years, we protect our furry mortals. We steer them away from the "forbidden" foods and keep them on strict diets for their own good. But in those final days or hours, the rules change. There is a profound, bittersweet healing in watching a dog who has lived on kibble finally experience the glory of a double cheeseburger or a vanilla cone.

If it is safe for them in their final moments, let them taste the "human things." A tiny piece of chocolate for a dog who has never known it, or a lick of tuna juice for a cat, is a way of saying, *The rules are gone; there is only love now.*

A Tour of Favorite Places

If your pet is still mobile enough to enjoy the car, take a "legacy lap." Visit the park where they caught their first frisbee or the creek where they always got a little too muddy. If they aren't up for the walk, simply sitting with them on a blanket in the grass of their favorite sunspot is enough.

The goal isn't activity; it's presence. It's the smell of the air, the feel of the wind on their face, and the comfort of you being right there beside them. These moments become the "memory anchors" you will hold onto long after they are gone.

The Living Celebration

We often wait until a pet has passed to gather and share stories of their greatness. I encourage you to consider a **"Celebration of Life"** while they are still here to enjoy it.

Invite the "inner circle"—the friends, family, or even the favorite neighbor who always had a treat ready. Let them offer one last ear scratch, one last "good boy," and one last photo. Your pet may not understand the words, but they will absolutely feel the concentrated vibration of love in the room. This isn't a funeral; it's an honor guard for a life well-lived.

Finding Healing in the Doing

Creating a Joy List isn't just for them; it is a vital part of *your* grief process. It allows you to shift from a state of "waiting for the end" to a state of "celebrating the now."

When the time eventually comes, you won't just remember the medications or the vet visits. You will remember the look on their face when they tasted that first fry, the way the sun hit their fur in the park, and the overwhelming circle of love that surrounded them. **You are giving them a beautiful exit, and in doing so, you are giving yourself the gift of peace.**

Oliver

45 Furry Mortals

Financial Realism

Levi

Levi - My Only Boy

"Levi, (fka Cosmic Cuddle Cat, or Cosmo for short), was a very young gray tabby kitten, and showed up one morning in the engine compartment of his foster dad's car. No one knew where his mom or siblings were. He was a mystery. He'd been out on his own for a little while… maybe days, since he was a little thin, his ears were dirty, and his lip was cut, as if he scraped it. He was taken to a rescue, and in a matter of days, he won everyone over, had gotten a lot healthier looking, and proved to be one of the cuddliest kittens ever.

He was very shy with toys, so maybe he had never played before. He did love people and could not wait to be picked up. Eventually, he learned to play, loved chasing balls, and mastered his turbo scratcher.

Levi, (Cosmo), entered my life when I went to the rescue to look at possibly adopting a young female brown tabby kitten. While I was there, he caught my attention, was extremely friendly, and he came up to me while sitting on a bench with his loud purring and showing off his biscuit-making skills. I instantly fell in love with him, and I ended up adopting the brown tabby and this cute little guy with fur the color of a soft cloudy day.

Levi was my first male cat to come into my life. All my former cats were female, and when he joined the family, he had two sisters, one being the young tabby, along with a six-year-old Tortie, who didn't seem very interested in either kitten.

It turned out that of all my cats, Levi had more personality than any of the others. He was my clown boy, always making me laugh, and performing dangerous stunts such as walking along the second-floor railing looking over the foyer below, and jumping up onto the top of doors and other high places. He was my "quality control" inspector, for every single box or bag that entered the house. He would check each one inside and out making a game of hide n' seek for his entertainment. When he wanted me to play with him, he would drag his wand toys across the room or up the stairs, signaling to me that it was playtime. He loved rolling over on his back for belly rubs and that was never a trap. He was my gentle and loving and snuggle boy.

When Levi was about 10 years old, he started to develop health issues. The vets could not pinpoint exactly what was going on. He would get sick and hide for about 12 hours and then the next day, was perfectly fine. This only happened every few months and never lasted longer than a day at a time. A couple of years later, this same thing started happening more frequently. I took him to specialists for testing. Eventually they thought it was possibly pancreatitis or a nervous stomach. Nothing definite showed up on tests and his bloodwork was normal.

At age 13 he started losing weight and the issues seemed more serious. After trying numerous medications, the specialists thought it was cancer and set him up on chemo. He became weaker and thinner and it did not seem like the treatment was working. At the age of 14, he lost a lot of weight and became lethargic. At that time, I knew I had a decision to make. He no longer had quality of life. I contacted a vet who did in-home euthanasia. As hard as it was to let him go, it was his time. It's never easy saying good-bye, but this seemed more difficult… my only boy.

The energy inside my home was never the same again."

— **Jill, Levi's Mom**

Love Is Infinite, Bank Accounts Are Not

I was deeply affected by the story of my elderly neighbors, a sweet couple who lived simply and adored their young cat, Jasper. Jasper was barely three when he was diagnosed with a rare, complex, chronic condition requiring constant specialized care, medication, and, potentially, an expensive, life-extending surgery. The veterinarian was kind, explaining the available treatments, but when the cost estimate came, my neighbors' faces went ashen.

They looked at their savings, then at their limited monthly income, and then at Jasper. Though they had a chance to buy him more time and comfort, the financial barrier was absolute. They had to make the heart-wrenching choice to say goodbye then and there, knowing full well that treatment was available, but simply out of reach.

That moment, when love clashed with economics, underscored for me that compassion must include financial realism.

Because of that story, I know I would be remiss—utterly failing the mission of honoring our furry mortals—if I did not address the stark, painful reality of the financial concerns surrounding comfort and hospice care.

Providing compassionate, dignified end-of-life care for your beloved furry mortal is an immense act of love. This commitment, however, comes with financial considerations that require honest, careful planning during the active phase of decline. Understanding the cost structure of hospice and comfort care is essential for making informed, non-urgent decisions during this deeply emotional time.

Acknowledging these financial limits is not an admission of a lack of love; rather, it is a profound exercise in responsibility. When we allow ourselves to be honest about what we can afford, we shift the focus from a frantic search for funds to a focused pursuit of comfort. Financial realism allows you to establish a ceiling of intervention, where you decide in advance which treatments are sustainable and which would cause a level of financial distress that might compromise the peace of the household.

By setting these boundaries early, you protect yourself from the guilt of the possible—the haunting feeling that you should do more simply because a medical option exists. In the end, a pet does not measure the cost of their care; they measure the quality of the presence beside them. A home filled with calm, affordable care is infinitely more valuable to a dying animal than a home filled with the silent, heavy tension of a financial crisis.

The core message is this: financial realism is necessary to create a compassionate care plan that ensures costs do not compromise the pet's dignity. **While love is infinite, bank accounts are not, and sometimes, the best decision for a pet's comfort is brutally limited by cost.**

Proactive Financial Planning

The emotional journey of end-of-life care for a pet is often compounded by significant financial stress. Prolonged care, specialized medications, and supportive therapies can be very costly, and the expenses associated with veterinary visits, special diets, and treatments can quickly accumulate. We are driven by immense love but love alone cannot pay for comfort care. **To ensure your ultimate decisions are guided by compassion and dignity, not cost, the time to plan is *now*, when your furry mortal is still bounding and bright.** Financial foresight is the ultimate act of preventative love, removing the stress of money so you can focus only on comfort when the emotional crisis hits.

Laying the Financial Foundation: Four Preemptive Acts of Love

The goal is to build a financial safety net before the first sign of decline. Here is how you proactively secure your pet's future dignity:

Establish a Dedicated Dignity Fund: Do not rely solely on general savings. A powerful act of preparation is to establish a savings account specifically designated for future veterinary or end-of-life expenses. Treat this Dignity Fund like an emergency account you hope never to fully use. By setting aside even a small amount regularly, you create an immediate financial buffer. This fund ensures that when a terminal diagnosis arrives—sudden and shocking, as Oliver's was, you have immediate funds available for diagnostics or initial comfort measures without having to panic or sacrifice your pet's immediate needs.

Proactively Review Your Pet Insurance Coverage: If you have pet insurance, use a quiet afternoon now to pore over the details, not when you are weeping in a clinic lobby. Understand exactly what your policy covers for chronic or terminal conditions, as opposed to accident-only coverage. Check the fine print on deductibles, limits for specific diseases (like cancer or kidney failure), and, most critically, any pre-existing condition clauses. Knowing your coverage limitations today allows you to plan around them tomorrow. If you do not yet have insurance, researching policies now—while your pet is still young and healthy—is the best way to secure future coverage for late-life illnesses.

Pre-Research Charitable Avenues and Aid Options: Knowledge is power, especially when time is short. Become familiar with the charitable landscape now, so you aren't desperately searching for a lifeline during a crisis. Research national non-profits like The Pet Fund and RedRover, which are dedicated to helping pet parents afford care for chronic or terminal illnesses. Keep a clear, accessible list of these organizations, along with their application criteria, as a part of your larger Crisis Protocol (discussed in Part 11). Understanding where financial aid might be available eliminates chaos in the future.

Understand Payment Flexibility and Resources: While payment plans and credit options are typically negotiated during a crisis, knowing the available mechanisms beforehand is essential planning. Research third-party credit options specializing in veterinary costs and understand whether your regular clinic offers in-house payment options. Being aware of these flexible resources ensures that you have payment avenues ready to deploy instantly, allowing your focus to remain entirely on your pet's comfort and quality of life.

By taking these preemptive financial steps, you transform the financial burden from a sudden catastrophe into a manageable element of your pet's life plan, ensuring their dignity is guaranteed to the very end.

The Landscape of Care Costs

When you receive a terminal diagnosis for your beloved pet, your world narrows to one thing: providing comfort. However, the costs associated with advanced diagnostics, chronic pain management, hospice care, and the final farewell quickly become a massive, unspoken stressor. You cannot ignore or minimize this reality, as financial constraints force heartbreaking decisions on loving pet parents.

My goal here is not to offer financial advice, but to clearly outline the typical financial landscape of end-of-life care so you make informed choices without added panic.

The path you choose determines the cost of your pet's final journey, making it essential to understand the financial differences upfront.

The Phases of Ongoing Care

When you first suspect an illness, advanced diagnostics often represent the highest initial costs. This involves specialized blood work, X-rays, ultrasounds, and consultations with specialists like oncologists or cardiologists. You pay these costs to get a definitive picture of your pet's condition.

Once the path shifts to palliative care, the expenses become recurring and long-term. This commitment is centered on managing pain and symptoms to ensure comfort. Financial planning must account for the ongoing cost of medication, which can include daily, long-term drugs for pain management (like NSAIDs or Gabapentin), anxiety, or underlying conditions such as heart or kidney failure. Beyond prescriptions, you must also factor in costs for therapeutic diets, supplements, and practical mobility aids—things like supportive slings, non-slip mats, or even custom-fitted wheelchairs, all designed to improve your pet's quality of life during their final chapter.

The Final Farewell: Euthanasia and Aftercare

The costs associated with the final act—euthanasia—are generally more predictable but fluctuate significantly based on setting.

Choosing an in-clinic setting is typically the lower-cost option. You transport your pet to the veterinary hospital for the procedure. In contrast, in-home euthanasia offers the immense comfort of saying goodbye in your pet's most familiar and peaceful environment, but this convenience comes at a higher price. Mobile veterinary services charge a travel or house-call fee in addition to the base procedure fee, making it a notably more expensive, but often more therapeutic, experience.

The aftercare plan is the single biggest determinant of the total cost. If you opt for communal cremation, the service provider cremates your pet alongside other animals and scatters the ashes; you do not receive them back. This is the least expensive option. Choosing individual or private cremation means your pet is cremated alone, and their ashes are carefully returned to you in an urn or scattering box for memorialization, which is a significantly more substantial financial investment. Should you choose burial, costs vary from zero (if burying at home, where permitted) to a substantial fee for a plot at a pet cemetery. Regardless of the choice, most vets offer memorial items like paw prints or fur clippings as small, personalized add-ons.

The financial journey of end-of-life pet care is not a single cost, but a fluid progression of expenses, starting with recurring, long-term costs for diagnostics and palliative comfort, and culminating in a final farewell cost heavily determined by the choice between an in-clinic or personalized in-home setting and the type of aftercare selected.

Pet Insurance - The Pre-Existing Condition Cliff

For many pet parents facing end-of-life decisions, pet insurance either acts as a financial lifesaver or causes deep frustration. You must understand how policies typically work regarding chronic and terminal illness.

Most pet insurance policies rely on the concept of pre-existing conditions, and this clause presents a major hurdle. If you purchased the insurance after a veterinarian recorded your pet's diagnosis (or after the mandatory waiting period expired), the insurance company will likely deny all claims related to that specific illness, even years later. Once a pet receives a terminal diagnosis, the policy will likely place all future treatments, diagnostics, and palliative care for that condition under the pre-existing clause.

However, this does not render your policy useless. Even with a pre-existing terminal condition, insurance is structured to cover unrelated illnesses or accidents. For example, if your geriatric dog with cancer suddenly breaks a leg, the insurance should cover the emergency orthopedic surgery and recovery for the broken leg, since that is a separate, unexpected event. Additionally, some specific policies may cover the cost of humane euthanasia, but you must call your provider to confirm this.

This is why we strongly recommend you act immediately: if you have pet insurance, call them at once after receiving a diagnosis. Be direct and ask:

- "Is this condition considered pre-existing?"
- "What is my maximum lifetime payout for this condition, if any?"
- "Does my policy cover in-home euthanasia?"

Navigating the fine print of insurance is not merely a financial task; it is an act of advocacy for your pet's peace. By resolving these clinical and fiscal questions early, you reclaim your role as their emotional anchor rather than their medical bill manager.

When we are looking for pet insurance, whether when we get a new puppy or when it is time for renewal, we always check on the "lifetime payouts" for conditions that we have dealt with before or that we know are breed specific.

This clarity allows you to move away from the stress of "what can we afford?" and toward the much more meaningful question of "how can we best honor them?" When the logistical boundaries are set, you create a protected space where the final chapter can be written in the language of love and dignity rather than fine print and deductibles. It ensures that when the time comes to make the most difficult choices, your mind is clear, your heart is present, and your focus remains exactly where it belongs: on the gentle spirit of the companion who has walked beside you.

Financial Resources

When the emotional weight of a diagnosis is compounded by the inability to pay, it is vital to remember that resources exist. You are not alone, and there is support available to help your pet receive the care they deserve.

Programs to Finance Veterinary Bills

There are several financing options specifically designed to help cover large veterinary expenses. The most common is CareCredit, which functions like a credit card for healthcare. We used CareCredit for emergency medical treatments like Zack's spontaneous pneumothorax and Oliver's spleen removal. This option is accepted by many veterinary practices and offers special financing plans that allow you to pay off a significant bill over several months, often with a period of interest-free repayment if paid in full on time.

Foundations and Assistance Funds

Beyond standard financing, numerous charitable organizations offer grants and funds to cover veterinary bills, particularly for unexpected or end-of-life care. These funds are typically reserved for those facing financial hardship and are paid directly to the vet clinic. Organizations like The Pet Fund help with non-basic, non-emergency veterinary care, while Red Rover Relief often focuses on urgent and immediate critical care needs. It's always worth checking with local assistance resources, such as breed-specific rescues, your regional Humane Society, or local veterinary colleges—these groups frequently run limited funds or low-cost clinics for advanced care, recognizing the burden these costs can place.

Negotiating with Your Clinic

Do not hesitate to have an honest conversation with your veterinary team. They are compassionate people who understand the financial pressures involved. Ask if the clinic offers an in-house payment plan for established reliable clients. You can also discuss a phased treatment schedule that spreads the cost out over time, perhaps by focusing only on essential comfort measures (the palliative-only path) rather than pursuing a high-cost, low-probability curative treatment. Finally, for ongoing medications, ask if they can provide a prescription you can fill at a human pharmacy (like Walgreens or Costco). Using discount programs like GoodRx at these locations can sometimes drastically reduce the long-term, recurring cost of essential drugs.

No pet parent should have to sacrifice their pet's comfort or miss out on their final days of companionship due to the crushing weight of cost; resources exist because love is priceless and help is available.

furry mortal

[noun]

A beloved creature of spirit and fur whose life is measured in seasons rather than decades, reminding us that the depth of a bond is not defined by its duration.

Pre-Planning for Peace

Zack

Zack - The Right Goodbye …
and the Hardest

"While the previous personal stories have explored some painful lessons learned from difficult goodbyes, this is a story that illuminates the path toward a peaceful and dignified transition.

These experiences, though still steeped in sorrow, offer a profound sense of peace and the strength needed to heal. They represent the ideal outcome of a holistic approach to end-of-life care, where compassion, informed decision-making, and open communication guide every step.

For us, that ideal was embodied in our beloved Zack, our "one." **Zack was a magnificent 17-year-old Border Collie**, a dog who was truly more human than dog and he knew it. He had been with us through so many chapters of our lives, a constant, intelligent, and devoted presence.

Zack was this little smooth border collie in a cage at a local pet supply store staring up at us. He was the only one in the cage as all of his litter mates had been lost to Parvo, but Zack survived … he was a fighter since day one. We knew the minute we picked him up to hold him that he was coming home with us. The name they had given him was Thunder, we would come to realize why. The booming of his bark, for such a small thing, would shake the house.

Zack loved a good swim, just a lap or two and in a very planned manner. And no other dog had better disturb his laps, not even his brother, Oliver. And his favorite toy, much to our dismay, was the Kong tennis balls that squeaked. Although he loved to destroy a good stuffed toy in 2 minutes every holiday, everyone knew to send a package of those balls as well. We can still hear that squeaking and it always brings him back to me.

When the time came for us to consider his final journey, we were determined to "do it right" by him, applying the lessons we'd learned from past experiences. Zack had lived a wonderfully long and full life, filled with adventures, puzzles, and countless shared moments. But even for a dog as spirited as Zack, age began to take its toll.

His ability to get up on his own was slipping, his once-graceful walk became more labored, and the joy he found in simple activities was slowly fading. He was still able to walk into the veterinary clinic that day, a small but significant detail that reflected our commitment to prioritizing his comfort and dignity.

The day we said goodbye to Zack was, without a doubt, the toughest decision we have ever made. But it was also undeniably the right one. Our veterinarian, Dr. Jane, who had cared for Zack since he was a puppy, was incredibly caring and compassionate. The entire clinic, in fact, mirrored her empathy. Dr. Jane walked us through every step of the process, ensuring we understood what to expect and that Zack remained calm and comfortable. Saying goodbye to our special boy was tremendously hard, leaving a void that could never truly be filled. Yet, knowing with absolute certainty that we had made the right decision for him—choosing peace over prolonged decline—gave us the strength we needed to begin the long, slow process of healing.

Zack's peaceful farewell solidified our belief that a well-managed, compassionate end-of-life journey is the greatest gift we can give our cherished companions."

— **Angela & Laurel, Zack's Moms**

The When, Where, and Who

The moment I truly understood the necessity of pre-planning for a pet's end-of-life journey was when I realized how fundamentally different their experience of suffering is compared to ours. As humans, we can weigh the long-term benefits of temporary suffering, like going through chemotherapy, because we can anticipate that the future might be better. **But for our furry mortals, there is only the quality of life** *now*. They are wholly consumed by their pain and cannot anticipate that tomorrow might be better. That profound difference is what makes pre-planning for a pet so much harder.

The end-of-life journey for our beloved companions is one of the most difficult experiences we will ever face. By facing this preparation now, it can become an act of deep compassion that transforms decision-making from an emotional crisis into a path of foresight. My goal with these chapters is simple: to give you other options to help ensure that when your pets final moments arrive, you can think, "*I have no regrets*", because you separated the logistical burden from the acute grief of the moment.

The first step in this pre-planning process is to confront the hardest question: the **When.** It is essential to have an open, honest conversation with your veterinarian about the anticipated progression of your pet's known condition or age-related decline. You need a medical baseline; a set of clear markers that define their subjective quality of life before suffering becomes constant. Discussing this now, when your pet is still having more good days than bad, allows you to determine what you, and your veterinary partner, agree constitutes the "tipping point" for their unique personality. Write down these specific, non-negotiable markers—such as the loss of interest in a favorite person, the inability to eat unassisted, or chronic, unmanageable pain—because those written, objective truths will be your anchor against the tidal wave of emotion when the time is near.

Now we must address the practical and emotional setting for the final farewell: the **Where.** We have explored the benefits of at-home euthanasia and specialized facilities, and now is the time to select and document your preference. Research a local in-home euthanasia service, such as those recommended by organizations like Lap of Love, or identify a dedicated, serene end-of-life facility in your area. Have their contact information clearly recorded and share it with your family and a trusted emergency contact. By pre-selecting the environment, you eliminate the frantic research and decision-making during a time of crisis, guaranteeing your pet's last moments are spent in the most comforting, peaceful setting possible, whether that is their favorite sunbeam at home or a tranquil, non-clinical room.

The final piece of this logistical puzzle involves securing your support system: the **Who.** This goes beyond merely listing your emergency contact in the Crisis Protocol. It is about pre-determining who in your immediate circle you want present, and who you want to handle the specific tasks that follow. Be completely honest with your loved ones about your wishes. Do you need a friend to be the one to physically transport your pet's remains for cremation? Do you want a family member to take your surviving pets out of the room before the euthanasia begins, sparing them the distress? Do you wish for your regular veterinary clinic to handle the aftercare, or have you chosen to work directly with an aquamation provider? **These small, forethought logistical decisions transform the chaos of grief into a quiet, organized ritual of remembrance.**

By establishing the When, Where, and Who ahead of time, you honor your pet's final chapter with the clarity and compassion they deserve, **ensuring your love is perfectly executed to the very end.**

The Compassion Contract

Preparing for your pet's end-of-life journey demands more than just legal documents and emergency numbers; it requires profound emotional preparation, what can be called the compassion contract. This is a deeply personal commitment you make to your pet and yourself, rooted in the philosophy of prioritizing their present-day dignity over your future grief. This work allows you to engage in a necessary process of pre-grieving, which, while emotionally challenging, acts as a necessary counterpoint to the reactive decision-making of a medical crisis. By allowing yourself to feel the loss now, you liberate yourself to act with rational, selfless compassion when your pet needs you most.

Pre-grieving is simply acknowledging and processing the impending finality of your time together while your pet is still present and comfortable. It means recognizing that the love you share will soon be a memory and deliberately shifting your focus from hoping for a cure to maximizing quality time. **One of the most powerful ways to honor this contract is by creating a legacy list, a non-medical version of the care plan. This list is a deliberate inventory of the small, simple joys that define your pet's good day.** For a dog, it might be a short, gentle car ride to smell the ocean air; for a cat, it could be a shared cuddle session with a favorite, smelly blanket. By intentionally scheduling and savoring these final, authentic moments of happiness, you build a treasure trove of positive memories that will sustain you through your future grief, rather than solely recalling the distress of their final days. This proactive pursuit of joy is an indispensable component of the compassion contract.

This emotional pre-planning must include a clear-eyed look at the potential for caregiver burden; a topic already explored in this book. Your compassion contract is with your whole family, which includes your own well-being. By determining the financial and emotional boundaries you cannot cross—such as repeated, stressful emergency visits that only prolong suffering, or the financial strain that risks your own emotional health, you create a compassionate safety net for yourself. This is not selfish; it is sustainable.

When the unavoidable decline arrives, your pre-established boundary, the promise to yourself not to sacrifice your pet's comfort for an extra day of fear, will be a non-negotiable guiding light. This proactive, emotional preparation allows you to detach the overwhelming love you feel from the difficult medical decision you must make, ensuring that your pet's peaceful passing is truly a final, selfless act of pure, unadulterated love, free from the heavy weight of last-minute guilt and regret.

Securing the Time We Don't Have

The hardest part of loving a furry mortal is knowing that one day, we will be absent. Whether through illness, accident, or simply the passage of time, the moment we can no longer reach out and touch them will arrive. Our senior pets, those wobbly, medicine-requiring souls, rely on the predictability of our presence. Planning for their continued well-being after our departure is not morbid; it is, in fact, the final, most profound act of *being present*. It is the ultimate unburdening of worry.

When I first learned the scope of the problem—the sheer number of cherished, beloved pets who end up in the shelter system immediately following a parent's death—I was shocked and saddened. It is a staggering statistic, a betrayal of the deep, silent promises we make every time we stroke their aging backs.

For a senior pet, this vulnerability is amplified. A seven-year-old dog with early arthritis or a twelve-year-old cat with kidney disease cannot simply "re-home" seamlessly. Their survival depends on consistency, specialized diet, medication timing, and a very specific kind of quiet comfort.

We must accept a painful legal truth that runs contrary to our hearts: in the eyes of the law, your furry mortal is personal property. This is the obstacle we must overcome. Because property cannot be a beneficiary, leaving money and a request in a simple Will often fails. The funds may be released to a caregiver, but without legal oversight, the care itself becomes a mere suggestion, easily discarded in the face of financial pressure or changing priorities.

We need something stronger, something that acknowledges them not as property, but as *family*—a document that carries the weight of a sacred promise. **We need to build two bridges: one for the instant, sudden emergency, and one for the long, permanent journey.**

1. The Crisis Protocol

The moments immediately following a person's incapacitation or death are pure chaos, and in that chaos, our senior pets are often forgotten. The formal processes of a Will or Trust take weeks, sometimes months, to activate. We cannot let our companions go unfed or untreated during that gap. This is where the Crisis Protocol—the immediate bridge—comes in.

You need to select someone you trust implicitly, a Designated Caregiver, who lives nearby and holds a key. But more importantly, this person must hold a single piece of paper: a Written Authorization for Emergency Veterinary Care.

It is the most practical form of love you can offer. If you are unconscious or unreachable, this document tells the veterinarian, "Yes, this person is authorized to approve emergency surgery or medication *now.*" This one step eliminates the tragic hours lost waiting for legal permission to save a life.

We must also be honest about the cost of that immediate gap. The Executor of your estate will be overwhelmed; they won't be able to access the main funds instantly. Your Crisis Protocol must be accompanied by instructions—an explicit directive in your Will—to allow your Executor to immediately pay for all short-term care, boarding, or veterinary expenses. We cannot ask a loving friend to assume a massive financial burden simply for stepping in during our darkest moment. That immediate funding is the grease that keeps the transition smooth and compassionate.

2. Perpetual Care for Pets

For long-term, legally enforceable care, we must move beyond the Will and establish the Pet Trust. Think of this not as a legal burden, but as the Ultimate Guardian Contract. It is the only way to transform your heartfelt wishes into legally binding mandates, ensuring your dog's specialized diet continues for years or that your cat's insulin schedule is never missed.

The genius of the Trust is that it separates the love from the money, creating a Board of Directors for your pet's life:

- **The Trustee (The Manager):** This person manages the money. They are the investment steward, making sure the funds are protected and only disbursed for the care you specified. They don't have to live with the pet.

- **The Caretaker (The Heart):** This is the person who lives with the pet, provides the day-to-day love, and follows your instructions for their comfort and routine. They send the bills to the Trustee.

- **The Enforcer (The Advocate):** This is perhaps the most critical role. The Enforcer is a third party with the legal right to check on the Caretaker. If the Caretaker decides to cut corners or neglects the pet, the Enforcer has the authority to step in, take legal action, and place the pet with a new, more responsible guardian.

This structure eliminates risk. It ensures that the money is used only for the pet, and the quality of care is constantly monitored by an impartial advocate who holds your deepest wishes as law.

So, let's step back and look at this whole structure, what is truly the Ultimate Guardian's role? They become the person who sets the standard. The one defining our pet's lifestyle and detailing every little thing that matters, from their preferred blanket to their vet's name.

This whole setup isn't just about shuffling money; it's about making love and commitment to our beloved pet legally immortal. By choosing them I am building a fortress around my pet's future so that even when I'm gone, my voice and my wishes remain the law, ensuring their happiness and security are non-negotiable.

I've already chosen my Ultimate Guardian (for both the instant and long-term). **It wasn't about who had the most money or the biggest house; it was founded entirely on the love that person already has for my furry mortals.** I simply couldn't hand over this sacred responsibility to anyone who didn't already share a deep, existing bond with them. That relationship—that existing love—is the true, emotional foundation that gives the entire legal Trust its meaning.

The Dignity Clause (The Final Word)

The legal work is an empty vessel without the compassionate details we pour into it. Because senior pets come with predictable, high-cost needs—chronic illness management, specialized foods, comfort care—the funding must be generous and future-proof. You must direct your Trustee to factor in inflation; the cost of medicine five years from now will not be the same as it is today. This financial foresight is a necessary component of responsible love.

But the most important language we write in the Trust is the Standard of Care. **You must mandate that the Caretaker maintains "a quality of life consistent with that enjoyed during my lifetime." This is the heart of the document.**

And finally, the most tender, final instruction: the End-of-Life Decisions. To ensure a humane and dignified end, the Trust should be clear. It must prohibit euthanasia except when two licensed veterinarians agree that the pet is suffering irreversibly and has no reasonable Quality of Life remaining. This removes the decision from the realm of emotion or convenience and places it into the objective care of medical professionals, ensuring your pet is granted a peaceful release only when all other efforts have failed.

By meticulously planning for their future, we honor the contract we began the moment they came into our lives. We allow ourselves the peace of knowing that even when we are gone, our love, codified by law, will continue to keep them safe.

The actual paperwork and legal details can feel completely overwhelming. It's one thing to know we need to have all of this in place; it's another to actually manage all the details. I used an app called **EverAfter** (see Furry Mortal Resources) to make writing my wishes and will so much easier. It turns something huge and scary into something genuinely manageable. And it can be easily updated as things change, which in the pet world they do quite often.

Oliver

Blending Approaches

Tootie

Tootie - The Power of Love & Compassion at the Vet

"Tootie was a one-of-a-kind dog—a true "Heinz 57" mutt with the heart of a lion. A mix of cattle dog, beagle, and who knows what else, she started life in a heartbreaking way, found in a trash can with her litter mates. The lid had slammed shut on her tail, leaving the tip permanently gone.

Despite this rough start, Tootie was a force of pure joy and endless energy. Her world revolved around making people happy and playing fetch until she was completely worn out. She was only 11 years old, and her energy seemed boundless, which is why her sudden decline was so alarming. We rushed her to the vet, where we learned the devastating truth: she had acute kidney failure from ingesting coolant from an outdoor air conditioning unit.

We managed her condition for as long as we could, even though she hated her new kidney-friendly diet (and Tootie LOVED to eat!). But eventually, the disease took its toll. Tootie's energy vanished, and we took her to Dr. Jane for help. They kept her for a few days, giving her fluids and monitoring her vitals, hoping to find a path forward.

That Friday, we were told we could bring her home with a new medication. By this point, her breathing was labored, but we were holding onto hope. Tootie was a fighter, and we wanted to give her the weekend to see if the new medicine could help.

But on Monday, we had to make the hardest decision of our lives. Her breathing had worsened, and she was fighting for every single breath.

It was time to say goodbye. We scheduled her final appointment for that evening.

We spent her last day doing all her favorite things. She laid on her favorite beds on the deck, enjoying the sun and eating all the treats she wanted. She even had one last burst of her old feisty self, jumping up to give the trash men a proper scolding.

Carrying her into the clinic that evening was the most difficult thing I've ever done, but I knew it was the right choice. She passed away peacefully in our arms, surrounded by love. We left her wrapped in her favorite blanket with her most cherished toys. Dr. Jane was an incredible source of comfort, guiding us through our first "decided" goodbye with immense compassion. Her kindness made a terrible time a little more bearable.

The way those final hours are handled can make all the difference in the world, they can be the start of healing or a source of lasting pain. To all the veterinary professionals who understand this truth, may you always have the strength to be there for families in their hardest moments."

— Angela, Tootie's Mom

Creating a Sanctuary at Home

The minute you walked into our house you knew we had a senior pet. Runners on the hardwood floors, sheets on the sofas and chairs, steps to get up on them, raised food and water bowls, a bed in every room for comfort. We had it all.

Zack (our border collie who lived to be 17) needed all the help he could get the last year of his life and we provided it. His mobility was diminished as his hearing was, so we made sure everything was set up for his comfort. We even made notes on all our delivery service apps to NOT ring the doorbell as we have a senior dog. We could always tell how grateful he was for the support as he stayed on the runners when walking and used all the extra beds and steps, we put out for him. **He was a proud dog ... but being so super smart, he also knew his limitations.**

For senior and terminally ill pets, the home environment plays an important role in their comfort, safety, and overall quality of life. Making thoughtful modifications to their living space can significantly improve their well-being during their final stages.

Providing comfortable and supportive bedding is paramount. Orthopedic beds or extra padding can help alleviate pressure points and provide relief for pets with arthritis or limited mobility. Ensuring easy access to food and water is also essential. Raising food and water bowls can be beneficial for pets with neck or back pain, allowing them to eat and drink in a more comfortable position.

Modifying flooring for better traction can prevent slips and falls, especially for pets with weakness or balance issues. Placing rugs or non-slip mats on hardwood or tile floors can provide the necessary grip.

For pets that have difficulty navigating stairs or getting onto furniture, providing ramps or steps can make a significant difference in their independence and comfort.

For cats, optimizing litter box accessibility and design is important. Using litter boxes with low sides can make it easier for cats with mobility issues to enter and exit. Creating quiet and safe spaces to rest is key for reducing stress and providing a sense of security. This could be a comfortable bed in a low-traffic area where the pet can retreat when needed. Maintaining a comfortable temperature and adequate ventilation in the home is also important for overall well-being.

Beyond physical modifications, routine and familiar surroundings provide significant emotional comfort for pets, especially as they age or their health declines. Maintaining a predictable schedule for feeding, walks (if still possible), and interaction can provide a sense of normalcy and security. Familiar scents and objects, such as favorite blankets or toys, can also be comforting. It is also important to minimize stressors in the environment, such as loud noises, sudden changes, or disruptions to their routine.

Creating a comfortable and accessible home environment is an important aspect of providing holistic end-of-life care for pets, directly impacting their physical and emotional well-being. Simple modifications can significantly improve a pet's comfort, reduce pain, and increase their ability to navigate their surroundings, contributing to a better quality of life. Stress and anxiety can be exacerbated by an unsuitable home environment, further compromising a pet's health and well-being at the end of life.

Providing a calm, predictable, and secure environment can help reduce anxiety and promote relaxation, positively impacting the pet's overall comfort. By actively adapting their home environment, pet parents can take a proactive role in enhancing their pet's comfort and peace during their final stages, fostering a sense of control and contributing to a more positive end-of-life experience. This active participation can also be emotionally beneficial for the caregiver, providing a tangible way to express their love and care.

Checklist: Creating a Sanctuary at Home

Creating a comfortable and safe home environment is a cornerstone of compassionate end-of-life care for your pet. This checklist is designed to help you transform your space, focusing on your pet's physical and emotional comfort during their final stages.

Comfort & Rest

- **Provide supportive bedding:** Use orthopedic beds or extra padding to alleviate pressure points and provide relief for arthritis or limited mobility.

- **Create quiet, safe spaces:** Designate low-traffic areas with comfortable beds where your pet can rest without being disturbed, promoting a sense of security and peace.

- **Maintain a comfortable climate:** Ensure the room temperature and ventilation are comfortable for your pet, as their ability to regulate their body temperature may be diminished.

Mobility & Safety

- **Improve floor traction:** Place rugs or non-slip mats on hardwood or tile floors to prevent slips and falls, especially for pets with weakness or balance issues.

- **Install ramps or steps:** Use ramps or pet stairs to help your pet access their favorite furniture or navigate stairs, allowing them to maintain a sense of independence.

- **Optimize litter box accessibility (for cats):** Use litter boxes with low sides to make it easier for cats with mobility issues to enter and exit.

Food, Water & Hygiene

- **Ensure easy access to food and water:** Raise food and water bowls to a comfortable height for pets with neck or back pain, allowing them to eat and drink without strain.

- **Maintain a clean environment:** Keep your pet and their living areas clean to prevent discomfort and infection.

Emotional & Mental Well-being

- **Maintain a predictable routine:** Stick to a consistent schedule for feeding, walks (if possible), and interaction to provide a sense of normalcy and security.

- **Use familiar scents:** Surround your pet with familiar objects like their favorite blankets or toys, which can provide emotional comfort.

- **Minimize stressors:** Avoid loud noises, sudden movements, or disruptions to their routine that could cause stress or anxiety.

By using this checklist, you can create an environment that addresses your pet's changing needs, ensuring their final days are as comfortable and peaceful as possible. **Providing holistic end-of-life care for our senior or terminally ill pets requires transforming their home environment to maximize their physical comfort, safety, emotional security, and overall quality of life.**

Balancing Care

Choosing the best course of care for your beloved companion, integrating the gentle support of holistic therapies with the necessary strength of conventional medicine—should be an informed decision, not an emotional reaction. Your veterinarian is your partner, but you are the expert on your pet's soul, and together, you form the only team capable of navigating this complex path.

Understanding the Goals of Care: It is essential to clarify your goals right from the start. Are you still seeking a cure, or has the mission shifted entirely to maximizing comfort and joy? Have an open, honest conversation with your care team about your pet's prognosis and the reality of the treatments. Ask this: *"Are we buying time, or are we buying quality of life?"* Your answer guides everything that follows.

Open Communication with Your Veterinarian: Your veterinarian is your partner in navigating these choices. Have open and honest conversations about your pet's condition, prognosis, and all available treatment options, both holistic and conventional. Ask questions about the potential benefits, risks, and costs associated with each approach.

Considering Your Pet's Individual Needs: Every pet is unique, and what works well for one animal may not work for another. Consider your pet's personality, temperament, and how they have responded to different treatments in the past. Some pets may tolerate medications easily, while others may be more sensitive. Some pets may enjoy gentle touch therapies, while others may find them stressful.

Integrating Approaches: It is helpful to create an integrative approach that combines the strengths of both holistic and conventional medicine. For example, you might use pharmaceutical pain medication to manage severe pain while also incorporating massage therapy for relaxation and acupuncture for additional comfort.

Considering Quality of Life: Throughout the decision-making process, always keep your pet's quality of life at the forefront. Regularly assess their comfort level, ability to engage in enjoyable activities, and overall happiness. If a treatment, whether holistic or conventional, is causing more distress than benefit, it is time to reconsider that treatment.

The Pivot Point: A Framework for Shifting to Comfort Care

I understand the desperate hope that makes us cling to curative treatments, even when they seem to be failing. I did this with Lucy, prioritizing longevity until we reached a crisis point that left me with profound regret. To prevent that heartbreaking outcome, you need a formal framework for recognizing the when the struggle outweighs the joy. At that exact moment your courageous love should shift your focus entirely from cure to comfort. This is the hardest, but most selfless, decision you will ever make.

Here is a formal, step-by-step framework for making that courageous pivot, explicitly using the objective data you collect in Part XIII:

1. **Anchor Your Decision in Objective Data:** Your first step is to use the Furry Mortals QOL Assessment Tool (Chapter 13) as your ultimate anchor. The emotional pull to continue fighting is immense, but the data you are tracking for Mobility, Happiness, and Pain is factual. If the overall numerical score drops consistently below the established "Questionable" threshold, or if key metrics like Pain or Appetite score the lowest marks, you have objective evidence that the current path is unsustainable.

2. **Identify the Point of Diminishing Returns:** Review your daily tracking. Are the repeated vet visits, the new medications, or the uncomfortable diagnostics truly restoring

a meaningful level of joy and comfort? If your Good vs. Bad Day Calendar shows that the bad days consistently outnumber the good ones over a period of seven to ten days, this is your undeniable sign. The returns on curative efforts have diminished, and they are now causing more distress than benefit.

3. **Formalize the Conversation with Your Care Team:** Bring your completed QOL assessment and your Good vs. Bad Day Calendar to your veterinarian. This data transforms the conversation. Ask directly: *"Based on these objective metrics, is the primary goal of this conventional treatment still a cure, or are we now prolonging suffering?"* This initiates the formal shift in medical strategy.

4. **Execute the Comfort Shift:** Once you and your veterinarian agree that the Point of Diminishing Returns has been reached, you must commit to the full shift to comfort care. This means immediately ceasing any aggressive, high-stress, or low-impact diagnostic or curative treatments. Focus every resource—emotional and financial—on ensuring pain management and maximizing comfort for the remaining time. Your goal is no longer fighting the disease; it is preserving their dignity until the final goodbye.

5. **Trust Your Instincts:** As your pet's primary caregiver, you know them best. Trust your instincts and advocate for their needs. If something doesn't feel right, don't hesitate to seek a second opinion or explore alternative options.

By carefully considering these factors and working closely with your veterinarian, you can make informed choices that **honor your pet's well-being and provide them with the best possible care during their final stages of life**.

Vet Medicine's Role

Although the main focus of this book is from a more holistic approach to end-of-life care for our pets, we have to be very aware that a comprehensive approach to end-of-life care often combines the strengths of both holistic and conventional veterinary medicine to provide the most compassionate support for our beloved pets. **All of my furry mortals have had a combination of both, holistic and conventional treatments, at their end-of-life.**

Conventional veterinary medicine plays a vital role in providing comfort and managing symptoms for pets at the end of life. Conventional treatments often focus on directly addressing the physical ailments and discomfort a pet may be experiencing. Let's explore some of the key ways conventional medicine can support end-of-life care.

- **Pain Management with Pharmaceuticals:** Veterinarians have a range of pharmaceutical options for managing pain in pets, including non-steroidal anti-inflammatory drugs (NSAIDs), opioids, and other analgesics. These medications can be helpful in alleviating suffering and improving a pet's comfort when holistic methods alone may not be sufficient. Veterinarians can tailor pain management plans to the individual pet's needs, considering the type and severity of pain.

- **Management of Specific Illnesses:** Conventional veterinary medicine offers treatments for managing the symptoms of various diseases common in older pets, such as heart disease, kidney disease, and cancer. This might include medications to manage fluid retention in heart failure, dietary management for kidney disease, or chemotherapy to slow the progression of certain cancers. While these treatments may not be curative, they can significantly improve a pet's quality of life in their remaining time.

- **Nutritional Support:** Veterinarians can recommend specific diets or supplements to address nutritional deficiencies or support organ function in ailing pets. In cases where pets have difficulty eating, veterinarians can guide parents on assisted feeding techniques or recommend feeding tubes to ensure adequate nutrition.

- **Fluid Therapy:** Dehydration can be a significant issue for pets nearing the end of life. Veterinarians can administer subcutaneous or intravenous fluids to help maintain hydration and support organ function, improving comfort and overall well-being.

- **Surgical Interventions:** In some specific cases, conventional surgery might be considered to improve a pet's comfort at the end of life, such as removing a painful tumor or addressing a condition causing significant distress. These decisions are made on a case-by-case basis, carefully weighing the potential benefits against the risks and the pet's overall condition.

I want this book to be about balance. It's about taking the spiritual side of our deep bond—the love, the dignity, the focus on quality time—and pairing it with the clinical side of expert veterinary care. We must use every available resource, whether it's a cuddle session or a powerful prescription painkiller, to make sure our beloved pet's final chapter is as comfortable, peaceful, and meaningful as it can possibly be.

Food and Comfort

Appropriate nutrition plays a vital role in maintaining our pets' energy levels and supporting their essential bodily functions. As our pets age or their health declines, their metabolic needs may change, requiring adjustments to their diet. Easily digestible and palatable foods can encourage them to eat and maintain their strength. In some cases, under the guidance of our veterinarian, homemade diets or specific nutritional supplements may be helpful.

Maintaining proper hydration is equally significant for supporting our pets' organ function and ensuring their overall comfort. We can encourage their water intake through various methods, such as offering fresh water frequently, using pet water fountains, or adding moisture to their food. In some instances, our veterinarian may recommend administering subcutaneous fluids to supplement their intake.

Pets nearing the end of their lives may experience feeding challenges. Providing practical solutions, such as hand-feeding small, frequent meals or offering soft, easily palatable foods, can be helpful. In situations where our pet is unable to eat adequately on their own, the use of feeding tubes might be considered under veterinary guidance. Beyond the nutritional aspect, mealtimes and favorite treats can also provide significant emotional comfort and a sense of normalcy for our pets in their final days.

Proper nutrition and hydration are key to maintaining our pets' physical comfort and energy levels at the end of their lives, directly impacting their quality of life. Even when our pets' appetite is diminished, ensuring they receive adequate nourishment, and fluids can help maintain their strength and comfort. Difficulties with eating and drinking can lead to significant distress and a decline in overall well-being for our terminally ill pets.

As the goal of care shifts from longevity to legacy, our approach to nourishment must also evolve from strictly clinical to deeply compassionate. In these final stages, the strict rules of a senior diet or prescription kibble often give way to the "Pleasure Principle." If a pet's body is no longer able to process nutrients for long-term health, the nutritional data on a label becomes far less important than the light in their eyes when they taste a piece of roasted chicken or a lick of vanilla ice cream. This is nutritional grace—the understanding that a favorite flavor can be a powerful bridge to the present moment, anchoring a failing body in a brief, delicious sense of normalcy. By prioritizing their palate over their protein requirements, we honor their spirit, turning every meal into a celebration of the life they have lived rather than a reminder of the illness they are carrying.

Addressing these challenges with appropriate strategies, such as modifying food consistency or providing assisted feeding, can improve our pets' comfort and enjoyment of their remaining time. The act of providing food and water can also be a significant way for us to express our love and maintain a connection with our pets during the end-of-life journey, offering emotional comfort for both of us. **Even small gestures, like offering our pets' favorite treats, can provide moments of joy and connection during a difficult time.**

Healing Hands

Gentle touch therapies can offer significant comfort and pain relief for senior and terminally ill pets, providing valuable non-pharmacological options to improve their quality of life. Massage therapy, for instance, can help alleviate pain, promote relaxation, and improve circulation. Pet parents can learn simple techniques for gentle home massages to help their pets relax and ease muscle tension. Certified animal massage therapists can also provide more specialized treatments.

Veterinary acupuncture is another powerful tool for pain management, reducing inflammation, and promoting overall well-being. This ancient Chinese therapy involves inserting fine needles into specific points on the body to stimulate the release of endorphins, the body's natural painkillers, and to promote healing. Acupuncture can be helpful for a variety of conditions common in senior and terminally ill pets, including arthritis, chronic pain, and even nausea.

Animal chiropractic care focuses on addressing musculoskeletal pain and improving mobility through gentle adjustments to the spine and joints. This therapy can be good for pets experiencing gait abnormalities, stiffness, or pain related to arthritis or other musculoskeletal conditions. It is important to seek out qualified practitioners who are specifically trained in animal chiropractic. **Our dog Zack used to see a chiropractor regularly for his degenerative myelopathy.** He loved seeing Dr. Carolyn and he would bounce (yes, Zack bounced when he walked) out of the office saying hi to everyone along the way.

Gentle touch therapies like massage, acupuncture, and chiropractic care can play a significant role in enhancing comfort and managing pain in terminally ill pets, offering non-pharmacological approaches to improve their quality of life. These therapies can address musculoskeletal pain, reduce inflammation, improve circulation, and promote relaxation without the potential side effects of some medications. By stimulating the release of endorphins and other natural pain relievers, acupuncture and massage can help reduce a pet's reliance on pharmaceutical pain medications.

Oliver loved getting his cold-laser therapy and massage. He would put on his goggles and spend that time in a more relaxed state. His hip-dysplasia caused him a lot of discomfort, but he always found relief on his "spa day".

These types of treatments can be particularly beneficial for pets with organ dysfunction or those who are sensitive to medications. The growing integration of these complementary therapies into veterinary medicine reflects a more holistic approach to patient care, recognizing the value of addressing your pet's well-being through multiple avenues. **This integrative approach allows for a more personalized and comprehensive care plan tailored to the individual needs of your pet.** It is always recommended to consult with a veterinarian before starting any new therapy for your pet.

Supplements for Peace

Natural supplements are a powerful way to support our pets' health and well-being throughout their lives. Nature provides a wealth of resources that can be used to support comfort and manage various symptoms in terminally ill pets. Herbal remedies and nutritional supplements can offer gentle yet effective support for pain relief, inflammation, anxiety, and other common issues faced by aging and sick animals.

Throughout our pets' lives, we've found that natural supplements have been a cornerstone of our holistic approach to their care. We started early, giving our puppies and kittens fish oil for a healthy coat and probiotics for a strong digestive system. As they've gotten older, we've focused on supplements like glucosamine and chondroitin to support joint health and mobility, which was particularly helpful for Zack and Oliver. For our pets who have experienced anxiety or stress, we've seen noticeable improvements with calming supplements containing ingredients like chamomile or passionflower. We always discuss these choices with our veterinarians to ensure they are safe and effective.

When our cherished pets are dealing with age-related conditions, many of us look toward nature's gifts for supportive care. We've found that specific herbs and supplements can offer genuine, gentle relief.

For example, when joint pain or arthritis begins to limit their movement, compounds like Boswellia and turmeric are often used for their well-known anti-inflammatory properties. They provide a quiet, natural way to help manage discomfort and ease chronic stiffness.

Beyond easing physical discomfort, natural remedies can be profoundly helpful for a pet's emotional state. Herbs like chamomile and valerian are recognized for their calming effects, which can help reduce anxiety and stress, promoting a greater sense of peace as they near their end-of-life journey. These supports are available in various forms, including tinctures and capsules. Many parents also find that extremely gentle methods, like flower essences and aromatherapy, can be a comforting addition for emotional relaxation and support.

While these natural options offer profound support, it is critical to prioritize quality and sourcing, ensuring you choose reputable brands specifically formulated for pets. Above all, always consult with a veterinarian before administering anything new to a terminally ill pet. Your vet, especially if they have a background in herbal medicine, can provide personalized recommendations and advice on any potential interactions with conventional medications, ensuring safety and effectiveness.

Throughout our pets' lives, particularly as they face age-related and terminal illnesses, we used natural supplements to gently support their comfort, manage symptoms, and enhance their well-being.

Emotional Nurturing

As pets age or face terminal illness, they can experience a range of emotional and mental changes that significantly impact their quality of life. Cognitive dysfunction, similar to Alzheimer's disease in humans, can lead to disorientation, confusion, and changes in behavior. Pets may also exhibit increased anxiety and fear, becoming more easily startled or agitated. Some pets may experience depression and withdrawal, showing a lack of interest in their surroundings and becoming less interactive.

I saw this so clearly with my dog, **Zack**, who struggled terribly with what people call **"Sundowners Syndrome."** Just like in people, this is a behavioral change where pets get confused, anxious, or restless, and it almost always kicks in as the sun goes down. Zack's anxiety was gut-wrenching to watch; sometimes after he went out to potty at dusk, he would get completely disoriented and, instead of coming inside, he would hide right in the middle of the bushes, shaking and afraid to even approach the door. Our vet put him on anti-anxiety medication to help him get through this and it helped tremendously. These signs are a powerful reminder that care must include managing cognitive decline to ensure their final moments are spent feeling safe, not terrified.

Nurturing the emotional and mental well-being of senior and terminally ill pets requires a thoughtful and consistent approach. Maintaining a consistent routine and familiar environment can provide a sense of security and predictability, which is especially important for pets experiencing cognitive decline or anxiety. Providing plenty of gentle interaction and affection can offer comfort and reassurance.

Even if a pet is less responsive than they once were, quiet companionship and gentle touch can still be deeply comforting.

Engaging in gentle play and mental stimulation when the pet is able and willing can help maintain their cognitive function and provide moments of joy. However, it is important to respect their limitations and avoid pushing them beyond their comfort level. In some cases, a veterinarian may recommend the use of calming pheromones or supplements to help reduce anxiety and promote relaxation. And the potential benefits of animal-assisted therapy, such as visits from therapy dogs, should not be overlooked, as these interactions can provide comfort and joy.

A pet's emotional and mental well-being is just as important as their physical comfort at the end of life and significantly impacts their overall quality of life. Addressing anxiety, fear, and depression can improve a pet's sense of peace and security in their final days. Changes in physical health can directly influence a pet's emotional and mental state, and vice versa. For example, chronic pain can lead to irritability and withdrawal, while a loving and supportive environment can help a pet cope with physical limitations.

Nurturing the emotional and mental well-being of a senior pet strengthens your bond and provides opportunities for meaningful connections in their final moments. **Gentle interactions, familiar routines, and a loving presence provide comfort and reassurance to your pet as they face their end of life.**

Hard Choices

Lucy

Lucy - When Love Leads Us Astray

"When a beloved pet faces a serious illness, our immediate, overwhelming instinct is to fight for every single moment we can have with them. This profound love, however, can sometimes lead us down a path where our desire for longevity overshadows their quality of life. It's a difficult truth to confront but recognizing it allows for making truly compassionate end-of-life decisions.

We learned this lesson through the heartbreaking experience with our first pet together, a tiny cat named Lucy. **Lucy appeared on our doorstep, a fragile creature who immediately stole our hearts.** She was a delicate six-and-a-quarter pounds full grown, and from the start, her health presented significant challenges. Lucy was deaf, epileptic, and had a serious heart condition. Despite her ailments, she possessed an incredible spirit. She was happy, playful, and deeply loved, and we were determined to give her the best life possible.

Lucy was the most unique cat ever. When she would walk by anything reflective she would admire herself. And let me tell you, Lucy did not care about grooming herself at all. She was proud of her natural beauty! She loved to go into our atrium and sit in her favorite whiskey barrel in the sun for HOURS ... she would come in all sweaty with her hair a mess but happy as could be.

She was also known to wait for you come to her rescue rather than trying to rescue herself. One time she got wedged between a side table and the bed, and just stayed there until we realized she was stuck there. And this was from the top with feet dangling down ... her face was one of "woe is me". And being deaf, her meow was a just a tiny squeak so she was not one to howl out if in a predicament. Her laissez-faire attitude to life taught us to not take everything so seriously. She was more profound than she looked at her tiny size.

As Lucy's health declined, we found ourselves caught in the emotional maelstrom of wanting to do "everything" because we hadn't had much time with her. Our veterinarians, understandably, offered every possible intervention, and in our desperate love for Lucy, we accepted them all. She endured forced feedings to maintain her weight and multiple blood transfusions to combat her worsening anemia. Adding to her struggles, she developed breast cancer. Each treatment was a new battle, fought with the hope of extending her time with us, even as her body grew weaker and her daily comforts diminished.

The bitter end arrived during yet another blood transfusion. Lucy died without us by her side, a moment that compounded our grief with regret. In hindsight, we realize we chose the hope of longevity over quality of life, pushing her tiny body through aggressive treatments that, while extending her days with us, did not provide her comfort. That experience became a defining moment for us, a painful but invaluable lesson that has since shaped our approach to pet care.

It taught us that true love, in the face of terminal illness, sometimes means prioritizing comfort and peace over every possible medical intervention, ensuring their final moments are filled with dignity rather than distress."

— **Angela & Laurel, Lucy's Moms**

Advocacy in Action

When the time comes to consider hospice or comfort care for your furry mortal, the single most important step is initiating open, honest conversations with your veterinary team.

These discussions are essential for aligning medical possibilities with the core mission: preserving your pet's quality of life and supporting your family's profound emotional needs.

Do not wait for your veterinarian to introduce the topic of hospice—take the lead. At the first sign of a serious decline or terminal diagnosis, shift the focus by asking direct, courageous questions like:

- "Are we now focusing on comfort rather than cure?"
- "What hospice resources or specialists do you recommend in this area?"

Request a thorough quality-of-life assessment and be absolutely honest about what you are witnessing at home. It is immensely helpful to bring written notes tracking your pet's good days, bad days, and energy levels; these real-world observations are the data points that guide the best medical decisions.

Demand clarity on all available comfort care interventions. Ask your veterinarian to explain the options in accessible terms: *"What pain management protocols are appropriate for my pet's specific condition?"* and *"How will we objectively know if the current approach is truly working?"* Request a written care plan that clearly outlines all medications, realistic expectations, and the definitive signs that will indicate the plan needs adjustment. This is also the time to address practicalities, so don't hesitate to ask about the costs and time commitments involved in the different approaches.

You know your pet best; your veterinarian knows the medical science best. Together, you form the ideal care team. To ensure a smooth journey, establish clear, preferred methods of communication—be it scheduled calls, email updates, or tele-health check-ins. Share your pet's unique personality and preferences so the care remains personalized and respectful. If you ever feel rushed, unheard, or unsupported, remember that seeking a second opinion from a veterinary hospice specialist is a valid and powerful act of love.

As the time for end-of-life decisions approaches, ask your veterinarian to walk you through what to expect both physically and emotionally. Discuss all euthanasia options before they become an urgent necessity, including the feasibility and comfort of home euthanasia. Request guidance on how to sensitively explain the process to children or other family members. A compassionate veterinarian will help you balance the difficult medical realities with the profound necessity of honoring this final transition, ensuring your furry mortal's comfort remains the unwavering top priority.

Our pets give us their whole, pure hearts, and the greatest honor we can give them in return is to be their advocate. It means trusting your own gut when you know they're suffering and having the courage to speak up when things feel wrong.

This is the hardest work you will ever do as a pet parent, but when you champion their comfort and their dignity to the very end, I promise you will look back and know, without a doubt, that you did everything right.

Advocacy is ultimately about giving your pet a voice when they can no longer speak for themselves. While a veterinarian brings the stethoscope and the science, you bring the history and the heart. True advocacy means rejecting the one-size-fits-all approach to aging and insisting on a plan that respects your pet's unique spirit. It is the bravery required to say "no" to a diagnostic test that will only cause stress, or "yes" to a higher dose of pain medication that might make them sleepier but keeps them comfortable.

When you stand in that exam room and bridge the gap between clinical data and your pet's lived reality, you are doing more than just managing a case; you are protecting a legacy. This partnership ensures that the final decisions made are not just medically sound but are deeply aligned with the personality and the dignity of the animal you love.

Let's make this final chapter a beautiful, peaceful testament to the extraordinary love you share.

Trilogy of the Soul

This is the ultimate clarity tool for every pet parent. Our pets have their top three joy markers, the three activities that define their joy.

On a sticky note, in your phone's notes or on a sheet of paper that you can keep with you, list your pet's **Top Three Joy Markers**. These are not just biological functions; they are the soulful rituals that make your companion who they are.

Example:

1. Chasing the blue ball.
2. Eating peanut butter.
3. Sleeping on the velvet rug.

The Threshold

When your pet can no longer do, or no longer enjoys, **two out of these three things**, the mortgage of the heart is likely coming due.

This is not a failure of medicine or a failure of your love. It is a profound signal from their spirit that they are ready to let go of the physical world. As their advocate, your role shifts from the stewardship of their life to the stewardship of their peace.

Persistent grace means honoring this signal and choosing to carry the weight of the final choice you must make as your own, so that they may leave this world while their dignity is still intact.

"I am not ending their life; I am ending their suffering. My readiness to say goodbye is not a requirement for their need to go."

The Dignity of Pet Comfort Care

When our furry mortals face chronic illness or the natural decline of old age, our focus must shift from striving for a cure that is no longer possible to ensuring their comfort and dignity. This is the philosophy of comfort care: a profound, specialized approach designed to relieve suffering and maximize the joy they can still find in their remaining days with their family.

Comfort Care (also known as palliative care) is a compassionate contract you make with your pet. It represents an intentional shift, where the entire veterinary team focuses on quality of life over quantity of time. This approach is deeply respectful, acknowledging that when facing irreversible health challenges, a pet's emotional and physical comfort matters more than any aggressive, painful treatment.

The veterinary team develops a customized plan that centers entirely on the pet's unique personality and preferences. This means treating the whole companion—addressing pain management, ensuring nutritional needs are met, and supporting mobility, all while keeping their contentment as the core goal.

Effective comfort care is a seamless blend of medical science and thoughtful home adjustments. It relies on a strong pharmaceutical foundation: utilizing precise pain medications, anti-nausea drugs, and appetite stimulants to manage symptoms. Simultaneously, physical support is critical: investing in orthopedic beds, setting up ramps, and learning assisted feeding techniques. The most vital component, however, is the regular quality-of-life assessment. This ensures that the care plan remains flexible and is constantly adjusted to align with your pet's changing needs and comfort levels, guaranteeing that suffering is minimized.

Comfort care benefits pets with progressive conditions—like cancer or organ failure—where a cure is off the table. It is particularly invaluable for families who simply need time to prepare emotionally, offering peace of mind that their furry mortal is secure and comfortable during this transitional period.

Implementing a comfort care plan is a team effort requiring honest collaboration between you and your veterinarian. It starts with open conversations about realistic expectations, followed by regular check-ins to adjust medications and support measures. Many families find strength in maintaining a daily journal, tracking their pet's good moments, appetite, and energy levels to guide ongoing decisions about their quality of life.

Choosing comfort care is perhaps the most profound commitment you can make to your pet during their final chapter. While emotionally challenging, it brings the immense solace of knowing you honored their life by ensuring every possible comfort measure was provided right up to the end. The presence of veterinary social workers or pet loss counselors can offer necessary emotional support as you navigate this difficult but deeply meaningful caregiving journey.

The philosophy of comfort care for chronically ill or aging pets represents a profound, compassionate shift from pursuing an impossible cure to prioritizing and maximizing the pet's comfort, dignity, and quality of life.

The Gentle Transition to Pet Hospice

When a cure is no longer viable for our beloved furry mortals, hospice care provides a compassionate alternative, a philosophy focused entirely on comfort and maximizing quality of life. This specialized approach ensures our pets live their final days with dignity, allowing them to experience a gentle transition while their human family is supported through the wrenching emotional journey.

Pet hospice is not about giving up; it is a philosophy of care that consciously prioritizes comfort over cure for animals facing terminal conditions. Unlike the often sterile environment of emergency care, hospice centers on managing symptoms and cherishing the human-animal bond through the pet's natural decline. Specially trained veterinary teams become partners with families, working together to create highly individualized care plans. These plans honor each pet's unique personality and specific needs, guaranteeing they are never without solace.

A comprehensive hospice program focuses on transforming the pet's familiar home environment into a sanctuary. It combines robust pain management through targeted medications with practical support, such as mobility assistance (using slings or carts) and nutritional support tailored to their changing abilities.

The true value of hospice is in the education provided to families: learning to recognize subtle signs of discomfort and mastering the techniques for gentle nursing care at home. Regular quality-of-life assessments become the guiding light, helping families monitor their pet's condition and make informed, compassionate decisions about care adjustments when the time eventually comes to consider the final transition.

Organizations like the **AHELP Project - Animal Hospice, End of Life, and Palliative Care Project** (see Furry Mortal Resources) are central to this movement, working to prepare, guide, and empower pet parents through their animal companion's journey—during illness, end of life, and beyond—to make compassionate decisions that promote quality of life. They embrace a core mission of adapting human hospice principles for pets, focusing on awareness, education, and compassionate support for pet parents. AHELP offers personalized Animal Hospice Coaching and Comprehensive Care Calls to help families confidently navigate their pet's end-of-life care. They help pet parents by providing resources such as a guide with over 40 questions to ask their veterinary team, helping them understand their pet's diagnosis and proceed with hospice care, and ensuring they create thorough plans and back-up plans to avoid spur-of-the-moment, distressed decisions.

Hospice care emphasizes keeping the pet in familiar surroundings, relying on simple, effective home modifications to increase comfort. Families learn how to create safe, cozy spaces using orthopedic bedding, easy-access litter boxes, and non-slip mats. Essentially, the approach encourages meaningful, quiet interactions—gentle grooming, favorite small foods, and steady companionship that respects the pet's often dwindling energy levels.

Choosing hospice is an act of reclamation; it is the moment you reclaim your pet's final chapter from the cold urgency of medical intervention and return it to the warmth of the home. This transition marks a profound shift in the household's energy—moving away from the frantic anxiety of "saving" and into the sacred stillness of "honoring."

In this space, the ticking clock of a terminal diagnosis is replaced by the steady rhythm of a shared afternoon nap or the quiet comfort of a hand resting on a familiar head. Hospice grants you permission to stop fighting a battle that cannot be won and instead start a vigil that is defined by peace. It ensures that your pet's final memories are not of the antiseptic smell of a clinic or the prick of a needle, but of the soft light of their favorite room and the steady, loving presence of the person who has been their entire world.

Quality hospice programs understand that caring for a dying pet impacts the entire family. They offer counseling resources, guidance on memorial planning, and bereavement support to help families process their complex emotions.

This holistic care creates the space for necessary goodbyes, ensuring that our furry mortal experiences a peaceful, gentle transition surrounded only by the deep love of their family.

The Ultimate Hard Choice

Mia

115 Furry Mortals

Mia - Echoes of At-Home Euthanasia

"The decision to offer a pet a peaceful passing at home is, for me, the ultimate act of love and compassion. I simply can't imagine saying goodbye anywhere else after having to make that call in the vet office or animal hospital too many times before. At-home euthanasia services are invaluable, providing a gentle alternative to the often-stressful clinic environment. These organizations are truly fabulous, bringing dignity and serenity to a difficult moment.

However, I've learned that even with the best intentions and the most compassionate care, the process itself—and its lasting impact—can hold unforeseen challenges if you aren't fully prepared beforehand.

I experienced this firsthand with my beloved cat, Mia. **Mia was such a vibrant and loud member of the family.** She would talk non-stop until she had been fed and never missed a meal. She loved to give kisses and to have her picture taken. She was the epitome of a brown tabby through and through. And a tiny one at that … my other cats had always been big cats, but Mia was tiny and stayed tiny her entire short life. I rescued her with her brother Levi whose story I have shared as well.

My little Mia took a turn for the worst all of a sudden … she was battling persistent fevers and overwhelming lethargy, her quality of life rapidly diminished. Recognizing her suffering, I made the decision to call an at-home euthanasia service. I wanted Mia's final moments to be in the comfort and familiarity of her own home with me.

The veterinary team arrived, professional and empathetic, ready to facilitate Mia's peaceful transition. I was holding Mia in my lap as the veterinarian administered the sedative. The drug's effect was rapid and profound, causing Mia's muscles to relax completely and unexpectedly. I was shaken when the sedative took hold. Mia went limp so quickly that her sudden weightlessness caused her to fall out of my lap onto the floor.

The memory of this incident has become an unexpected trigger, replayed in my mind and it made my grief process so much more complex. While the service was invaluable in bringing peace to Mia, the lack of preparation for such a physical response from the sedation left an emotional wound that persists.

My experience with Mia has taught me a critical aspect of compassionate at-home euthanasia: the absolute necessity of being completely upfront about what will occur. This includes not only the step-by-step medical procedure but also the potential physical reactions of the pet, such as complete muscle relaxation or vocalizations, which can be alarming if unexpected. It highlights the importance of discussing the potential for *triggers*—sights, sounds, or even locations—that can be left behind and complicate grieving. A truly holistic approach to end-of-life care ensures that both the pet and their devoted human companions are as fully prepared as possible for every aspect of this profound final act of love.

Despite the painful moment with Mia, I want to emphasize that I use in-home pet euthanasia every time, without question. While the plan for Mia didn't occur as I expected, all my other pets have been able to pass away peacefully, at home, in their familiar environment."

— Jill, Mia's Mom

The "Rainbow Room"

The "rainbow room" at our vet's office has seen a thousand silent farewells, yet every time I walk in, it feels like the first. I've been there so many times, not just for my own, but to lend my shoulder to friends who couldn't bear the final walk alone. With every heartbeat, every gentle stroke of a fading coat, the truth becomes clearer: the greatest act of love is sometimes the release of control.

It began with my first dog, Tootie. For weeks, she fought. She slept with me, she guarded the house for me, she stayed for me, her little body battling an invisible tide. She wasn't afraid of dying; she was afraid of disappointing me by leaving. When I finally held her close, stroking her ears as the vet prepared the injection, I felt her trembling anxiety. But as the gentle fluid entered her vein, a profound stillness replaced the tremor. Her head settled heavy in my hand, and for the first time in months, her body, rigid with chronic pain, relaxed. It wasn't my choice alone; it was an acceptance she communicated in her tired gaze. In that moment, I understood the true meaning of the word peace.

Later, there was Zack whose spirit was too big for his arthritic frame. He'd try to wag his tail every time we came near, even though the effort always threw him off balance. He fought his pain with a loyalty that broke our hearts. When the time came, we laid on the floor with him, his head tucked under my chin. As his breathing softened, the years of fighting—the labored breaths, the struggle to rise—simply dissolved. His body became light and utterly tranquil. We felt the burden of his suffering lift, and in its place was a quiet, overwhelming gratitude that we could give him what no amount of medicine or desperate wishing could: dignity and rest.

In every instance—whether it was the dog who could not catch another breath, or the dog whose broken body had stolen his joy—the process was never about giving up; it was always about honoring their tireless fight. They fought for us, every single one of them, clinging to life out of that pure, unconditional love.

And yet, in the hushed aftermath, holding that suddenly still, warm weight, I have never once felt a pang of regret. My heart aches, yes, a raw, deep grief for the missing presence. But the regret? No. Because what I witnessed was the purest gift: a final moment of relief, delivered in a familiar embrace.

We are so fortunate, as guardians of these gentle, furry mortals, to have the ability to make this final, selfless choice. If we can end their struggle, replacing pain with immediate serenity, giving them the beautiful, quiet exit they deserve, why would we ever choose otherwise?

It is the final, profound act of compassion on our journey together, the ultimate acknowledgment that their peace matters more than our pain of letting go.

The Final Choice

In the final, difficult stages of a pet's life, the discussion of euthanasia can be framed not as a failure, but as the ultimate compassionate act— a direct application of Gawande's principles of prioritizing dignity and peace over the relentless pursuit of survival. Facing a pet with a significantly diminished quality of life, euthanasia offers a profoundly loving way to relieve pain or suffering that can't be fixed when other options are no longer effective. This understanding helps us address the common fears and guilt associated with the decision, allowing us to move forward with a sense of peace, knowing we are choosing our pet's well-being and dignity above all else.

Determining when it might be the right time for euthanasia is a deeply personal decision. Quality of life assessments can be a valuable tool in this process, helping parents to objectively evaluate their pet's overall well-being. Considering the pet's ability to engage in activities they once enjoyed, their level of pain and discomfort, and their overall demeanor are important factors. It is also extremely important to recognize when medical interventions are no longer providing meaningful improvement in their quality of life.

Understanding the process of euthanasia can also help alleviate some of the anxiety surrounding it. Parents often have the option of choosing between having the procedure performed at a clinic or in the comfort of their own home. Many parents find the option of at-home euthanasia to be a more peaceful and personal experience for both themselves and their pet.

It is common for family members to be present during the procedure to offer comfort and say their final goodbyes. But experience has shown that some people are not able to be there to see their beloved family member take their last breath. This is not weakness or lack of love; this is a testament to the depth of their love and there is no shame or judgement in whichever choice is made.

Be completely honest with yourself before making the decision of whether to be present or not ... the wrong choice can make the healing process last even longer.

Throughout the decision-making process, open and honest communication not only with yourself, but with a veterinarian or other end-of-life care specialist, is paramount. They can provide valuable guidance, answer questions, and offer support as you navigate this emotionally challenging time.

Euthanasia, when performed with compassion and care, is a final act of love that can prevent prolonged suffering in terminally ill pets. While emotionally challenging, it is often the most humane choice when a pet's quality of life has significantly declined and cannot be improved. Discussion and understanding are essential for navigating the complexities of end-of-life decisions, including euthanasia, ensuring that the pet's needs and your values are at the forefront. End–of-life care specialists can provide valuable guidance and support, helping you make informed and compassionate choices.

Delaying euthanasia when a pet is suffering can prolong their discomfort and diminish their final days. I (and others I know) have waited for a definitive sign or a "perfect" moment, but this can lead to unnecessary suffering for our beloved companions.

Euthanasia Explained

The first time I had to make this choice was with my dog Tootie, and my first question was (as it is with many pet parents), **"Is it painless?"** and it is the most important one for a loving pet parent facing this choice, and the simple answer is **yes**.

Euthanasia, which literally means "good death," is designed by veterinarians to be a peaceful, gentle, and painless procedure for your beloved companion. The goal is to allow your pet to transition without anxiety, distress, or discomfort. The process typically involves two main stages, ensuring comfort and a peaceful passing:

Sedation and Relaxation

In most cases, your veterinarian will first administer a sedative or tranquilizer. This injection is usually given into the muscle (intramuscularly) and feels like a routine vaccination.

- **What it does:** The sedative allows your pet to relax, letting go of any fear, anxiety, or pain they may be feeling. Within minutes, your pet will become very drowsy, calm, and often drift into a deep sleep. This ensures they are unaware of the final step.

- **Your role:** This time allows you to cuddle and comfort your pet while they become completely relaxed, saying your final goodbyes in a serene state.

The Final Injection

Once your pet is completely sedated and sleeping soundly, the veterinarian will administer the final solution. This is typically a high concentration of an anesthetic agent (often a barbiturate).

- **How it's given:** The solution is administered intravenously (into a vein), often through a catheter placed beforehand. This ensures the drug works rapidly and effectively.

- **What it does:** Because it's an anesthetic, your pet will not feel any pain. The large dose of the drug quickly travels to the brain, causing an immediate, deep unconsciousness. It then gently stops the heart and breathing. The process is rapid— usually taking only 10 to 30 seconds after the injection is complete.

What to Expect Right After

Once the injection is given, the veterinarian will use a stethoscope to confirm that your pet's heart has stopped. Though your pet is unconscious and gone, their body may exhibit a few completely normal, involuntary movements that can sometimes alarm parents. It is important to be aware that these movements are reflexes, and they do not mean your pet is in pain or aware:

- **Muscle Twitching:** Minor muscle tremors or twitches may occur due to nerve release.

- **A Gasping Breath:** You may see one or two final, deep breaths (called *agonal* breathing). These are brainstem reflexes.

- **Releasing bodily fluids:** As the muscles of the body relax completely, your pet may urinate or defecate.

- **Eyes Remain Open:** A pet's eyes generally do not close after death.

Knowing this beforehand helps prepare you so you can remain focused on your pet's peaceful passing, secure in the knowledge that they felt no pain.

Honoring Natural Passing

I've shared my own deeply held belief (a conviction born from sorrow) that the ultimate gift we can offer is a peaceful, planned farewell. I've shared with honesty that a *truly natural passing* is rarely peaceful and often ends in fear or unmanaged pain.

But your heart and your unique bond with your furry mortal may guide you down a different path. If your personal truth means choosing to stay home and support a natural passing without final veterinary intervention, that choice is rooted in immense love and a fierce commitment to your companion. That love deserves a protocol. This is not about judgment; it is about providing practical, absolute comfort that ensures your selfless decision brings dignity, not distress.

Comfort Focus: Creating a Sanctuary of Love

When the fight for a cure is over, your love shifts its focus entirely to comfort. This is your sanctuary contract—a deeply personal promise to wrap your pet in every physical and emotional solace you can provide.

1. **Prioritize Their Quiet Comfort:** Work with your heart and your veterinarian to establish a gentle, robust care plan. Even if you choose not to intervene to end their life, you must intervene fiercely to manage their pain. This involves using medications prescribed by your vet to keep them relaxed and comfortable, paired with the quiet comfort of your presence, gentle touch, and familiar scents.

2. **Make Their World Small and Safe:** Respect their dwindling energy. Move their favorite bed, water bowl, and food right

next to where they rest. Place soft blankets, non-slip mats, and gentle ramps exactly where they need them. Every effort you make to bring comfort to them is a profound act of service, ensuring they never have to struggle or be afraid in their own home.

3. **Be a Silent Anchor:** Your quiet presence is a medicine all its own. Some pets crave constant connection, leaning into you for reassurance. Others, in their final moments, retreat into quiet solitude. Be mindful of their subtle cues. Sit nearby, speak softly, and offer a gentle stroke only when they seek it out. You are simply their secure anchor in a changing world.

The Courage to Pivot: Recognizing Unmanaged Suffering

The choice for a managed natural passing requires a sacred responsibility: the courage to admit when that path is no longer serving your pet. We have to be brave enough to watch for the moment the suffering becomes too heavy—the point where your love demands a pivot.

You must look for the definite signs that the quality of life has dropped below the line of dignity:

- **Intractable Distress:** Severe, constant agitation or restlessness that cannot be calmed by medication or comfort measures. This is often accompanied by vocalizations (whimpering, crying) or frantic attempts to move, showing profound distress.
- **Difficulty Breathing:** Labored, forced breathing, constant panting while resting, or gasping for air. If they are struggling for every breath, their dignity is lost.
- **Constant Pain:** Pain that breaks through medication, causing them to flinch, shake, or guard their body aggressively, indicating they are in terror and chronic discomfort.

- **Unsettled Panic:** They cannot find peace, continuously shifting, pacing, or feeling trapped, showing they are fully consumed by fear.

If you observe these symptoms, your love requires one final, hard choice. Pivoting to urgent euthanasia is not a failure of your original conviction; it is the final, selfless act that upholds their dignity and prevents the unmanaged suffering you sought to avoid.

Post-Mortem Logistics: Final Acts of Service

When your furry mortal finally slips away, the moments that follow can be deeply confusing. These final, quiet tasks are your last act of service, helping you honor the body that held so much love.

1. **Gentle Positioning:** Move quickly and tenderly. Place your pet onto a blanket or towel and curl their body into a comfortable, sleeping position. This must be done within the first hour or two, as their muscles will naturally begin to stiffen (rigor mortis) soon after passing.

2. **Acknowledge the Changes:** As the body relaxes completely, you may see a release of fluids (urine or feces). This is normal. Use thick towels or puppy pads placed beneath them to manage this respectfully.

3. **The Cooling Process:** If you cannot immediately transport them to a crematory or burial site, the body must be kept cool to slow the natural process of change. Gently wrap them in their favorite blanket and place ice packs over their chest and abdomen. Store them in the coolest, quietest place in your home until transport is ready.

By embracing this protocol, you allow yourself to face this profound moment with confidence and peace. Your deep commitment ensures that, regardless of the path chosen, your pet's farewell is steeped in the dignity and unconditional love they deserve.

Pet Forward Goodbyes

When it's time to say goodbye to our beloved companions, we all want it to be as peaceful and comforting as possible. While our regular vets are wonderful, **there's a growing movement towards specialized end-of-life care facilities and in-home euthanasia services**, exemplified by companies like Honor Pet (see Furry Mortal Resources). These services are truly changing how we navigate our final farewells.

The heart of Honor Pet (and, hopefully soon, other services like it) is entirely centered on your pet's comfort and your family's peace of mind. Unlike a bustling general veterinary clinic, which must manage various appointments and emergencies, a dedicated end-of-life provider can offer a profoundly different experience. Imagine a serene, quiet space designed for comfort, not clinical procedures, or even more intimately, your own home, where your pet feels safest and most at ease.

In either setting, you'll be given ample time, without feeling rushed, before, during, and after the process, to say your goodbyes and process the moment. The entire approach is geared towards ultimate comfort. Beyond the moment itself, these services often seamlessly handle aftercare, such as cremation, and offer resources for grieving hearts.

While specific offerings may vary by provider and location, a comprehensive specialized service typically begins with the option for pre-planning. This allows you to speak with them beforehand about your pet's quality of life and thoroughly understand the euthanasia process, helping you feel prepared when the time comes. Many of these services specialize in in-home euthanasia, meaning a compassionate veterinarian comes directly to your home. This profoundly personal option allows your pet to remain in their most comfortable and familiar surroundings, minimizing stress for everyone involved and making the final moments deeply intimate. **Throughout the process, the emphasis is on a gentle and pain-free transition.**

Finding a compassionate and professional specialized end-of-life pet care provider in your area requires a thoughtful approach. Your trusted primary care veterinarian is often the best initial point of contact. They frequently partner with, or can confidently recommend, reputable in-home euthanasia providers or specialized facilities in your area, as they regularly work with these services to offer their clients more comprehensive options. Beyond your vet, online directories can be incredibly helpful. Organizations like the **International Association for Animal Hospice and Comfort Care (IAAHPC)** (see Furry Mortal Resources) maintain searchable lists of certified professionals dedicated to comfort care, which often include euthanasia services.

A simple online search using terms like "in-home pet euthanasia [your town/city]" or "specialized pet end-of-life care [your town/city]" will also likely bring up local providers. Take the time to visit their websites, read testimonials, and if possible, speak with them directly to understand their approach. And don't underestimate the power of personal recommendations; asking friends, family, or local pet community groups for their experiences can offer invaluable insight during such a sensitive time.

Following euthanasia, they will often take care of all aftercare arrangements for you, whether you choose cremation or burial, lifting that considerable burden during a time of immense grief. Many also offer various memorial options, from paw prints to personalized urns, providing tangible ways to cherish your pet's memory.

Choosing a "Pet Forward" goodbye is an act of sacred space-making. When we move the final farewell away from the sterile anxiety of a clinic and into the warmth of a living room or a dedicated comfort suite, we change the sensory imprint of the experience. Instead of the sound of barking dogs or the smell of antiseptic, the final memories are composed of familiar voices, soft blankets, and the scent of home.

This environment doesn't just benefit the pet by lowering their cortisol; it provides a soft landing for the grieving family. By ensuring the setting is peaceful, we prevent the trauma of a clinical crisis from overshadowing a lifetime of beautiful memories. It allows the final image in our mind's eye to be one of profound tranquility—a quiet, dignified departure that honors the deep love we shared, making the long journey of grief just a little easier to begin.

Choosing the right partner for this final journey can make all the difference, ensuring your beloved pet's farewell is as loving and peaceful as their life was.

Navigating the First 30 Days

The first day after the passing of a furry mortal is often characterized by a strange, hollowed-out silence. It is what sociologists call liminality—a threshold state where you are no longer who you were when they were alive, but you have not yet figured out how to exist without them. This is the "In-Between," a sacred and disorienting space where the muscle memory of years of caregiving meets the cold reality of a vacant home.

In these first thirty days, your brain will often play tricks on you, a psychological phenomenon known as searching behavior. You may find yourself glancing at the corner of the room where their bed used to be, certain you saw a flick of a tail. You might hear the tell-tale, hopeful "click-click" of nails on the hardwood, or pause in the kitchen, waiting for the weight of a head to rest on your knee. These aren't hallucinations; they are the protests of a heart that isn't ready to accept the silence. Your mind is simply trying to fill the "immense thing" that is the sudden absence of a constant heartbeat.

One of the most difficult hurdles in this first month is the geography of the home. Every water bowl, shredded toy, and stray hair becomes a landmine of memory. There is often profound guilt associated with moving these items. You might feel that by picking up the food bowl, you are erasing their existence, or that by vacuuming the rug, you are removing the last physical evidence that they were ever there.

To navigate this, I suggest a policy of gentle timing. There is no correct moment to put away their things. If the sight of the empty bed is too painful, move it. If removing it feels like a betrayal, leave it. You are the curator of this museum of love; you decide when the exhibits change.

The key to surviving the first thirty days is the creation of transition rituals. For years, your day was anchored by their needs: the morning walk, the evening feeding, the late-night bathroom break. When these anchors are pulled up, you may feel adrift. To find your footing, try to replace these caregiving routines with rituals of remembrance:

- **The Morning Light:** Instead of the morning walk, take your coffee to their favorite spot in the yard for five minutes of quiet reflection.
- **The Evening Candle:** At the time you usually served dinner, light a small candle next to their photo to honor the "joyful work" they completed.
- **The Memory Jar:** Whenever a sharp memory hits you during the day, write it down on a slip of paper and place it in a jar. This moves the pain out of your head and into a safe, physical space.

The first thirty days are not about getting over it. They are about surviving the silence. It is a period of intense emotional labor where you are learning to carry the missing hug. Be patient with yourself.

This quiet shift is the heavy price of the mortgage of the heart, but it is also where the foundation of your pet's lasting legacy begins to take root.

Grief Takes Many Forms

Zoey

Zoey - When They Decide for Us

"Sometimes, despite our careful planning and deepest intentions, our beloved pets make the ultimate decision for us, sparing us the agonizing choice of euthanasia. These unplanned farewells, while often peaceful for the animal, can leave a unique kind of grief for us, colored by the absence of a final embrace. Yet, in their quiet departure, there can also be a profound sense of peace and validation that we truly did all we could.

Such was the case with our Zoey, who truly was "that cat" for us. Zoey chose us when we went to get birdseed at a local pet supply store. She literally ignored every family that went by her cage until we walked by then she put on quite the show and it was immediate love.

She was an instant fit at home. Tootie and Liz, our two dogs at the time, took to her immediately. And that first night she already trusted us enough to fall asleep on my lap. Granted her tail never stopped tapping the entire time, but we soon realized that was normal for her. She was always a HUGE attention hog. She loved nothing more than a good party so SHE could be the center of attention. We loved to take her on walks outside using her favorite harness and leash. She loved to lay in the grass and fall asleep in a good sunbeam.

Zoey graced our lives for 15 wonderful years, a constant source of purrs, headbutts, and quiet companionship. Her health took a significant turn when she was diagnosed with congestive heart failure. It was a serious diagnosis, but working closely with our trusted veterinarian, Dr. Jane, we developed a comprehensive treatment and care plan. Through dedicated effort and expert guidance, we were incredibly fortunate to give Zoey five more years of truly good quality of life even after her diagnosis.

As the end drew closer, we noticed the subtle signs: she was sleeping more, her usual playful energy replaced by a quiet weariness. **We knew her time was coming, but true to her independent spirit, Zoey seemed to understand we could never make the final decision for her.** She took that burden upon herself while getting routine fluids.

We weren't fully prepared for the call, yet in our hearts, we knew it was a possibility. Our little girl passed away peacefully at the vet, surrounded by loving, caring people. While we have no regrets about Zoey's care or the extra years of joy we shared, a part of us will always wish we had been there with her, holding her in those very last minutes. In her passing, Zoey gave us a unique gift: the certainty that she chose her moment, sparing us the hardest decision, and leaving us with nothing but love and gratitude for the beautiful 15 years she shared with us."

— **Laurel, Zoey's Mom**

Grieving While They're Still Here

When Zoey was diagnosed with congestive heart failure, the end seemed eminent and there was nothing we could do about it. But we decided to try one more thing … non-invasive, just keep her home with us and keep her on routine medicine. One of us was with her around the clock. We monitored everything she did, eat, sleep, drink, cough, etc. During those late nights while she slept peacefully purring … I would cry knowing that no matter what we did … the end would come sooner than I wanted. I would hold her closer and her purring would increase. The love and bond growing stronger with every tear and every purr. The pain of the thought of that final moment was excruciating, but we put all of strength into pushing that final moment as far away as possible. It was all we could do. **Focus on the moment and live in it to fullest with her.**

This confusing, profound, and often guilt-ridden emotion is called **Anticipatory Grief.**

Most of society understands grief as something that happens *after* a death. But when we face a terminal diagnosis or watch a beloved companion decline, we start grieving immediately. It is the complex emotional reaction to an impending, inevitable loss. Naming this experience is incredibly important, as it helps us recognize that what we feel is real, valid, and a completely normal part of our shared journey.

What Does Anticipatory Grief Feel Like?

Anticipatory grief is often more complicated than post-loss grief because hope, denial, and the overwhelming responsibility of being a caregiver mix with it. It isn't a single state; instead, it manifests in many different and confusing ways for all of us.

We feel the simple, obvious sadness and mourning for the loss of our shared future, the walks we won't take, the morning cuddles we know will end. This sadness often partners with profound guilt and regret, where we might obsessively review past choices, wondering if we missed a symptom, waited too long for a diagnostic, or gave them the wrong food years ago. This process is our collective mind's way of trying to regain control over an uncontrollable outcome.

On tough days, we might feel impatient with our pet's accidents, or we withdraw from friends and family who don't understand the severity of our situation, because we are emotionally exhausted, and we have a low capacity for other concerns. This can escalate to a sense of desperation and bargaining; one moment we accept the inevitable, and the next we frantically research a miracle cure or specialized supplement, believing we can cheat the timeline.

To protect ourselves from the pain, we might unconsciously withdraw affection or attention from our pet, creating a painful distance before the actual separation. This emotional detachment is a defense mechanism, not a lack of love, but it often leads to profound guilt. Finally, worrying about the money spent, or the money *needed* to extend our pet's comfort, comprises a huge component of this grief.

Why Is Anticipatory Grief So Important to Validate?

Recognizing this type of grief offers two major gifts for our community: normalization and empowerment.

Normalization is the powerful realization that we are not being overly dramatic or morbid for grieving a pet who is still alive. Our hearts know the ending of this story, and they process the magnitude of that loss now, while our pet is still present. This demonstrates a deep, true attachment. This validation helps us lessen the guilt associated with our feelings. For instance, when we snap at a partner, or when we feel a strange sense of *relief* on a day when our pet finally rests peacefully, we understand that these extreme emotions are a product of stress and anticipatory loss, not a reflection of our commitment or love.

Empowerment comes from acknowledging this grief, which allows us to control our remaining time together. Instead of letting the looming future steal our joy, we purposefully shift our focus to what is still possible today. If we catch ourselves spiraling into worry about the inevitable decision of euthanasia, we must pull back and ask: "What does our pet need right now? What can we do in the next five minutes to give them joy?" This helps us create final positive memories. We must use this time actively; we should not let medical tasks solely dominate the last few weeks. Let's take photos, record videos of their funny quirks, and write down favorite memories. These acts of creation are incredibly therapeutic and build a well of comfort we can draw from later. Finally, when we feel overwhelmed by the task of medication schedules and cleanup, we consciously reframe the work: each pill we administer, each special meal we prepare, and each mess we cleanup is a final, irreplaceable act of love. This shifts the burdensome task into a profound privilege.

Anticipatory grief is painful, but it also provides a final gift. It is the deep, spiritual process that prepares us for the inevitable, allowing us to honor the bond while it is still physically present and ensuring that we spend our final weeks maximizing comfort and deepening our connection.

Grieving When They Are Gone

Caring for a senior or terminally ill pet is a deeply rewarding experience, but it also comes with significant emotional challenges. Pet parents often begin to grieve long before their pet's actual passing, a phenomenon known as anticipatory grief. This can involve a range of emotions, including sadness, anxiety, guilt, and even anger, as parents begin to come to terms with the impending loss. Understanding the stages and manifestations of grief, and recognizing the unique aspects of anticipatory grief, can help caregivers navigate these difficult emotions.

One of the most effective ways to navigate this difficult period is to practice self-compassion and emotional validation. It's essential to allow yourself to feel these emotions without judgment. Suppressing feelings of grief, pain, or fear can prolong the healing process, so giving yourself permission to mourn openly is a critical first step. By acknowledging your feelings as a natural part of the grieving process, you create a space for healthy emotional processing.

Tootie passed away peacefully in my arms in our vet's "Rainbow Room". She knew she was surrounded by love and she could finally let her worn out body rest. It was agonizing and peaceful at the same time. That same night, our neighbor was having a Christmas party and since we were new to the neighborhood he wanted us to come to meet people. We did not feel like celebrating anything. Then the doorbell rang, it was our neighbor wondering where we were. I told him about having to say goodbye to my dog Tootie and he looked at me and said, "*It is just a dog, you will get another one.*" and in that instance I learned exactly what disenfranchised grief felt like. Note: we are still friends, go figure.

The Invisible Pain: Addressing Disenfranchised Grief

There is a silent, isolating layer of pain that often makes pet loss uniquely heavy, and it begins long before the final goodbye. This trauma is called disenfranchised grief—the heartbreaking experience of having your profound sorrow minimized or dismissed by a world that sometimes fails to recognize the legitimacy of the human-animal bond, or the immense role your pet played in your life. When well-meaning friends or colleagues dismiss your pain with phrases like, "It was just a pet," or "You can always get another one," they are unintentionally invalidating your love and the magnitude of the relationship you shared. This external dismissal forces us to question our own feelings, making the pain feel lonely and illegitimate, which can aggravate and intensify grief experiences.

To protect your peace, you must first recognize that your feelings are valid, regardless of what the outside world suggests. Confide only in your trusted inner circle or seek out a dedicated support community—people who have also known the profound, silent presence of a furry mortal. You don't owe an explanation for your tears or your sadness to anyone who cannot see the true depth of your loss. Your self-compassion is your shield against this external judgment.

Finding a support system is another vital coping strategy. Caregivers often feel isolated in their grief, as not everyone understands the depth of the human-animal bond. Sharing your feelings with trusted friends or family members who have experienced pet loss can provide immense comfort and a sense of community. For many, joining a pet loss support group or reaching out to online grief support resources can be particularly helpful. One such resource is **The Parted Paw** (see Furry Mortal Resources). I found this service after I lost Bubba. The Parted Paw exists as a compassionate and certified support service, dedicated to ensuring that pets, their devoted parents, and pet care professionals navigating the complexities of loving an animal—

through care, grief, and the final goodbyes—never have to walk that path alone. They provide a safe space of understanding and empathy.

Another way to regain a sense of control and reduce anxiety is through proactive planning. Discussing end-of-life options with your veterinarian can help you make informed decisions when the time comes, whether it's managing pain, choosing the location for a final goodbye, or understanding the process of humane euthanasia. Planning for aftercare, such as burial or cremation, can also alleviate stress during an already emotional time. Beyond these practical arrangements, many caregivers find comfort in creating a "bucket list" of special activities to enjoy with their pet, from taking a favorite walk to sharing a cherished treat.

Finally, focusing on the present moment can be an incredibly powerful way to cope with anticipatory grief. Instead of dwelling on the future, shift your attention to the time you have right now with your pet. Engage in gentle activities they love, like a quiet cuddle on the couch, a slow walk in the park, or simply sitting together. These moments of presence allow you to create new, precious memories and reinforce the bond you share. **This focus on the here and now helps you cherish the remaining time and find joy in the little things, offering a beautiful counterpoint to the sadness of what's to come.**

Healing the Helper

Caring for a pet at the end of their life can take a significant emotional and physical toll on caregivers, leading to what is often referred to as caregiver burden. This burden can manifest as increased stress, anxiety, depression, fatigue, and a decline in overall quality of life. Recognizing the signs of caregiver burden is the first step in addressing it. These signs can include feelings of overwhelm, constant worry, fatigue, changes in sleep or appetite, irritability, and withdrawal from social activities.

Implementing self-care strategies is essential for managing caregiver burden. This includes prioritizing rest and sleep, maintaining a healthy diet, and engaging in activities that bring joy and relaxation. **Taking breaks and scheduling time for oneself, even for short periods, can help prevent burnout.** Seeking support from family, friends, or support groups can also provide valuable emotional and practical assistance.

Sharing the responsibilities of caregiving can significantly lighten the load. If you have other family members in the home, you can create a schedule to take turns with tasks like administering medication, feeding, or helping your pet get comfortable. Even small breaks can be restorative. For those who don't have family support, seeking respite care through a trusted friend or a professional pet sitter can offer you the opportunity to rest and recharge. These planned breaks not only prevent burnout but also ensure that your pet continues to receive consistent, loving care.

It's also essential to acknowledge and honor your own emotional needs throughout this process. Caregiving for a terminally ill pet is a profound emotional journey, and it's completely normal to feel a wide range of emotions, including sadness, anxiety, frustration, or even grief. Giving yourself permission to feel these emotions without judgment is a critical part of self-care. Recognize that it's okay to feel overwhelmed or exhausted, and that these feelings don't diminish your love for your pet. Being honest with yourself about your emotional state allows you to seek the support you need, ensuring you can be present for both your pet and yourself during this difficult time.

Healing the Post-Caregiver Void: The Loss of Purpose

The intense work of caregiving—the relentless schedule of medications, fluid therapy, special diets, and late-night checks—becomes a central purpose, defining our daily life and, often, our very identity. We poured our energy, focus, and love into sustaining that beautiful life.

When our pet passes, we face not only the crushing pain of loss but also a profound post-loss identity crisis. The pet is gone, but the caregiver role, the constant routine, and the central focus on management are instantly stripped away, leaving an emptiness that can feel disorienting and deeply isolating. This sudden void can aggravate our grief, making us feel lost, unneeded, or purposeless.

To navigate this difficult emotional shift, you must gently redirect the intense love and dedication you cultivated as a caregiver into new, meaningful routines and purposeful re-engagement. If you spent years meticulously focused on your pet's health, channel that energy into a new mission.

Consider volunteering your time or skills at a local shelter in their memory, helping another animal that needs compassionate care. This transforms your sorrow into a powerful, living tribute to your pet's legacy. Take the time previously dedicated to their demanding care—the hours spent on medication schedules or special feedings—and consciously reallocate it to nurturing yourself.

Use that time to establish new anchors in your life, whether it's dedicating an hour to a physical activity you enjoy, resuming a hobby you neglected, or connecting with friends.

By purposefully building new structures and finding a new avenue for your immense compassion, you prevent the void from consuming you, allowing the love for your pet to remain a source of strength rather than a painful memory of lost purpose.

Healing Through Memory

The loss of a beloved pet can bring profound grief and sorrow, a feeling that often catches us by surprise with its intensity. The deep bond we share with our animal companions makes them more than just pets; they are family members, confidantes, and sources of unconditional love. When they are gone, the silence they leave behind can be deafening, and the emptiness in our hearts can feel immense.

It's important to acknowledge that this grief is valid and to allow yourself the time and space needed to mourn. **You are not just grieving a pet. You are grieving a significant relationship, a daily routine, and a love that was a constant in your life.** This pain is real, and it deserves to be recognized without judgment.

Everyone's journey through grief is unique, and there is no right or wrong way to process this loss. You might find yourself cycling through a range of emotions—sadness, anger, guilt, and even relief—and all of these are a natural part of the healing process. Some people find solace in talking about their pet constantly, while others prefer to grieve in private. Some may feel the need to create a formal memorial, while others find comfort in quiet reflection. There is no set timeline for grief, so be patient and gentle with yourself. Your feelings are your own, and your path to healing will be too.

The grieving process following the loss of a cherished pet is a deeply personal journey, and there are many ways to navigate it and find comfort. One of the most powerful and healing approaches is to memorialize the pet, creating a lasting tribute to their life and the special bond you shared. This act of remembrance can take many forms, from tangible keepsakes to symbolic gestures.

For instance, you might choose to create a scrapbook or photo album dedicated to your pet, filling its pages with pictures, mementos, and notes that celebrate the joy they brought into your life. Another meaningful option is to plant a tree or a special garden in their honor. As the tree grows and the flowers bloom, it serves as a living memorial, a beautiful and enduring symbol of your love. For some, a memorial service or small gathering with family and friends can provide a space to share stories, mourn together, and celebrate the pet's life.

Beyond creating a physical memorial, many find solace in continuing the relationship through memories. **The love you shared doesn't end with their passing, and actively engaging with those memories can be incredibly therapeutic.** This can be as simple as spending time looking at old photos or watching videos of your pet. You might also find comfort in writing down stories or funny anecdotes, creating a personal narrative that keeps their spirit alive. Sharing these reminiscences with others who knew and loved your pet can also be a powerful way to process your grief and remember the happy times you shared.

Seeking support from others who understand pet loss, whether through friends, family, or support groups, can also provide comfort and a sense of community. Allowing oneself to experience the full range of emotions, including sadness, anger, and guilt, is a natural part of the grieving process. There is no set timeline for grief, and it is important to be patient and kind to oneself during this time.

And, when the time feels right, considering opening your heart to another animal companion can also be a way to honor the love and connection experienced with the pet who has passed.

The Weight of the "Should Have"

The ache of guilt is the unwanted shadow that often follows us after saying goodbye, feeling as heavy as the sorrow itself.

These complicated feelings stem not from any real failure in our care, but from the immense love and profound sense of responsibility we felt for our furry mortal. Learning to navigate this tender emotional terrain is a critical step in healing your own heart.

This painful "should have" feeling typically emerges from three sources deep within our grieving hearts. First, we often hold ourselves to impossible standards, believing we should have been perfect caregivers, catching every subtle sign and preventing the inevitable. Second, we torture ourselves by replaying medical decisions with painful, 20/20 hindsight—judging ourselves for information we simply did not possess in the moment of crisis. Finally, we magnify small, isolated regrets while tragically minimizing the vast, undeniable lifetime of unwavering love and comfort we actually provided.

The path toward peace begins with deliberate acts of self-compassion. **Start by creating a literal, tangible inventory of love—a simple list of all the ways you showed care**: the regular vet visits, the early morning cuddles, the specialty diets, and the favorite midnight treats. This evidence of care often helps balance the impossible perspective of guilt. Consider sharing this heavy emotional burden with someone who truly understands the depth of pet loss, whether through a support hotline or with empathetic friends and family. Many find comfort in creating a small, quiet daily ritual, like lighting a specific candle or visiting a memorial spot, to consciously maintain the precious connection with their companion.

While a degree of guilt naturally accompanies profound loss, there comes a point when professional support may be necessary. If, after several weeks, your guilt remains overwhelming, actively interferes with your daily life, or prevents you from remembering the love alongside the loss, a pet loss counselor or dedicated support group can provide expert guidance. Remember, seeking this help is not a sign of weakness; it is a profound act that honors your pet's memory as much as your grief does.

Your guilt is not a measure of your care, but a selfless testament to your love. The intensity of your pain demonstrates the true depth of your bond, a bond that was undoubtedly felt and cherished by your pet every single day.

Allow yourself to grieve without judgment and know that the enduring love you shared is the most powerful and beautiful legacy you leave.

Reflection 2

The Gift I Leave Behind

There is a specific vibration to the sound of a name when it is spoken by someone who loves you. To our furry mortals, that sound is a physical force, a spark that makes a tail thump against the floor or a tired head lift from a paw. In the early years, that name is called out across parks and through hallways, met with the bounding energy of a life just beginning. But as we enter the twilight of their journey, the name is whispered. It is spoken into the soft fur of a neck or breathed against a silver muzzle. In those quiet moments, we must realize that the bargain we struck was never about the quantity of time, but the quality of the light we shared. They came to us as a "candle flame," small but steady, accepting the gift of our life as their entire world.

As we navigate the end-of-life path, we often find ourselves living in the heavy silence of the "near miss." We sigh with worry that our pets can feel in the air; our fingers hesitate as they stroke the graying fur around their eyes, as if by slowing our touch, we could somehow "slow the hands of fate." We feel the weight of the mortgage of the heart, fearing the moment the debt comes due. But if we listen to the wisdom of the furry mortal, we hear a different message. They do not fear the transition. To them, the bargain was always fair. They do not tally the days remaining; they celebrate the "happy, wagging years" already banked. They are not focused on the sunset; they are focused on the fact that they are watching it with *you*.

Being a fierce advocate for your pet means adopting their perspective on the finish line. We see an ending; they see the completion of their "joyful work." The physical decline we witness is merely the shedding of a shell that has served its purpose. When that final softness falls and the spirit begins to roam, the love they cultivated does not simply vanish. It is not a thing that stops. Instead, it becomes a vast, invisible environment that wraps around us. The "broken piece" we feel in our chest, that jagged hole left by their departure, isn't a sign of failure. It is the "empty space" they have cast—a vessel now waiting to be filled with the legacy they left behind.

We often treat grief as a debt that love must now repay in suffering, but this book invites us to flip the script. The pain of losing a furry mortal is, in reality, the definitive proof of how much we won. You cannot have a hole that large without having first held a treasure of equal magnitude. Their unconditional legacy is the warmth that remains in the room long after they've left it; it is the way your heart has been permanently reshaped to be kinder, more patient, and more present.

As you stand on the threshold of saying goodbye, remember that your pet's work was to love you, and they did it perfectly. The sorrow you feel is the final stamp on a life well-lived. To honor them is to move forward not just with the memory of their loss, but with the light of their legacy. They leave us with a heart that is broken, yes, but it is a heart that has been expanded forever by the grace of a furry mortal.

Grief on Four Paws

Zander

155 Furry Mortals

Zander - When the Sirens Stopped Howling

"After we said goodbye to Oliver, every siren that came by sent a stab to the heart. Every missing deep sigh not heard when settling in for bedtime, broke it open again. But as we grieved, we noticed we were not the only ones feeling the pain from each of these. **Zander, Ollie's little brother, felt them too and even more profoundly.**

A little background on these two. Zander is just the opposite of our low-energy, big eater, sloppy kissing Bubba. He is a high-octane Texas Heeler ... but he was Bubba's devoted apprentice. A whirlwind of energy whose every move was dictated by Oliver's lead, sometimes much to Oliver's chagrin. Zander simply couldn't operate without Oliver's silent guidance. If Oliver decided it was time to nap, Zander napped. If Oliver ignored a noisy squirrel, Zander knew to ignore it too (and still does). They were a complete, if slightly mismatched, system.

When Oliver crossed the rainbow bridge, the sound went out of the house. There was no deep sigh next to the bed as he settled down to sleep, and the wail of the sirens passed by unacknowledged. The silence was immediate and heavy. We knew our loss was huge, but Zander didn't just miss Oliver; he had lost his navigator. His signature, boundless energy vanished, replaced by a low, anxious pacing. He was a ship without a rudder, and the sheer effort of deciding what to do next—where to lie down, when to drink water—was exhausting.

The loss became truly real when we brought Oliver's old, familiar harness home and laid it next to Zander on the large bed they had always shared. The harness smelled intensely of Oliver—his thick fur oily and sweaty, and love—yet Oliver himself was not there.

Zander pressed his nose into the thick nylon strap, and his sadness was palpable. He laid with the harness, resting his head next to it. His grief wasn't loud like Oliver's siren-howls; it was a profound, still ache that settled over him.

We recognized that Zander needed more than just comfort; he needed a lesson in self-reliance and stability. The world had become chaotic, so we immediately introduced the anchor of routine. Feedings, walks, and evening cuddle sessions were precisely maintained—a schedule we became religious about. This unwavering, predictable structure was a silent, powerful promise to Zander that the core safety of his life had not been lost, even if his partner was gone.

The task of filling the emotional void was a communal effort, and one that required patience. Every family member stepped in to be Zander's temporary anchor, ensuring he was never truly alone. This meant longer, focused one-on-one sessions: quiet time on the floor, lots of snuggling, and physical comfort he was missing from Oliver's solid, constant presence. We realized we needed that comfort too, finding solace in the rhythmic rise and fall of Zander's chest as we worked through our own sorrow.

But the most touching source of companionship came from Murphy the cat. Murphy, who also clearly missed the big, lovable Oliver, began seeking out Zander. When we returned home after being out, we often found the unlikely pair snuggled together—the grieving Heeler and the mournful feline—sharing silent, mutual warmth.

Slowly, almost imperceptibly, the joy returned. Zander started playing fetch again with true Heeler intensity, and his enthusiastic tail-wags were no longer strained. He still carries the memory of his Bubba—the echoes of a howl and the ghost of a shared sunbeam—but he now walks with a quiet confidence.

He found peace not by forgetting, but by being wrapped in the security of a family that saw his sorrow and taught his energetic heart how to trust its own path again."

— Angela & Laurel, Zander's Moms

Pet's Foresight

We focus intensely on the comfort of the pet who is leaving, but often we forget the silent observer: their best friend, the one who shares their water bowl and their sleep space.

Our surviving pets, especially those who have shared years with the departing one, understand the language of illness long before we admit it. **They know the rhythm of the house is failing.**

They smell the change in the chemistry of the body—the specific scent of disease, the weakness in the gait, the new vulnerability that requires closer proximity. The house is already beginning to feel different to them, a subtle shift in the gravitational pull of their world. This is their anticipatory grief, and it is a kindness to acknowledge it, to include them in the process of saying goodbye.

Maintaining the Anchor: As the life of the ailing pet shrinks—fewer walks, more quiet time, restricted movement—the routines of the healthy, surviving pet must remain as intact as possible. Your surviving dog needs his walk, even if it feels jarring to leave the other behind. Your surviving cat needs her usual play session. This consistency serves as an anchor, a quiet reassurance that the entire world is not dissolving. It allows them to maintain a sense of normal even as the atmosphere shifts around the ailing companion.

The Shared Farewell: The hardest but perhaps most merciful step is the choice regarding the final goodbye. If euthanasia is chosen at home, allow the surviving pet a chance to be present, or at least to encounter the body afterward. This is not for our comfort; it is for theirs.

When a pet simply disappears—taken to the clinic and never returned, the surviving companion is left without closure. Their world is incomplete, suspended in a state of searching. When allowed to gently approach the body after passing, they can confirm the death through scent. They understand the body is vacant. It may seem difficult to watch, but this moment of acknowledgment prevents weeks of confused searching and anxiety. It allows the surviving pet to begin their grief process grounded in reality, not bewilderment. This final interaction is a gentle way of communicating the truth.

The process of managing a pet's end-of-life journey must extend to the surviving companion.

The Echo of Absence

The silence after the door closes for the last time is deafening, and it is not just us who feel the lack. Grief in animals is often quiet, expressed through the sudden absence of habits that once filled the rhythm of the house. The surviving pet's search is heartbreaking: circling the empty spot on the sofa, standing vigil by the water bowl, or simply refusing to sleep in the shared bed.

Signs of Sorrow: Pay attention to the subtle shifts. A reduced appetite, changes in vocalization (unusual whining or silence), or an unexpected clinginess are common. Just as common, however, is a withdrawn pet who suddenly hides or sleeps excessively—a mirror of human depression. This is not misbehavior; it is sorrow. Their routine has been broken, and the primary source of their social structure is gone.

Patience and Presence: Our temptation is often to rush in and overcompensate. What the surviving pet needs most is patience and the return of their secure routine, now reorganized around a single individual. For the first few weeks, the focus should be on gentle reassurance and structure.

- **Scent of Memory:** Do not rush to clean or put away the deceased pet's favorite bed or blanket. The familiar scent is a comfort, a tangible memory that grounds them. Let them process the change in their own time.

- **One-on-One Attention:** Increase focused, positive one-on-one time with the survivor, but keep it low-pressure. If they crave a long walk or a favorite toy, offer it. If they prefer to lie silently at your feet, let them. The consistency of your presence is the medicine.

- **When to Worry:** If symptoms like refusal to eat, extreme lethargy, or anxiety (such as destructive chewing or sudden fear) last longer than a few weeks, consult your veterinarian. Sometimes, the emotional distress is so severe that behavioral modification or temporary, gentle medication is needed to help them re-establish their internal balance.

Grief is a slow journey of adjustment. The goal is not to force them to forget, but to help them find a new equilibrium where the memory of their friend exists peacefully within the new, quiet rhythm of their life with you. **It is a shared time of healing, demanding nothing but consistency and unconditional love from us both.**

Easing Their Grief

Our pets form deep social bonds, and the sudden, permanent absence of a companion can create a deep sense of confusion and distress in the surviving pet that requires our understanding and gentle support.

Animals express grief differently than we do, but their mourning is no less real. The signs often manifest as sharp deviations from their normal routine. You may notice subtle but significant changes in their behavior:

- **Appetite and Sleep Shifts:** Some pets may refuse meals entirely, while others may comfort-eat. Sleep patterns can change drastically—from sleeping excessively, often in their companion's favorite spot, to being restless and anxious throughout the night.

- **Searching and Waiting:** Many grieving pets will repeatedly search the house for their missing friend or wait intently by the doors and windows.

- **Social Changes:** They might become unusually clingy, seeking constant reassurance from you, or conversely, they may withdraw entirely, seeking quiet solitude.

These behaviors typically emerge within days and may persist for several weeks as your pet attempts to adjust to the profound disruption.

During this difficult transition, consistency and routine provide the emotional security your grieving pet desperately needs. Stability is compassion. Keep feeding times, walks, and play sessions on their normal schedule, even if your pet seems disinterested at first. Preserve their familiar sleeping arrangements unless they actively avoid the space. Maintaining clear household rules and boundaries prevents additional stress from changing expectations. The predictability of a stable routine is a powerful source of comfort when their world has been upended.

Animals benefit from opportunities to process the absence in ways they comprehend. If it is emotionally possible for you, allowing surviving pets a supervised moment to sniff a blanket or bed that carries the deceased's scent can help them register the loss without being overwhelmed. Use calm, reassuring tones when they are searching or showing signs of anxiety. For many, simply placing an item that carries their companion's scent in their sleeping area offers a comforting reminder. These quiet acts help them reach a degree of understanding about the absence.

Increase the amount of interactive play to stimulate positive emotions but always respect their clear need for quiet time. Engaging their minds with new puzzle toys or treat-dispensing games can help redirect anxiety. For pets struggling with anxiety, consider using calming pheromone diffusers or speaking with your veterinarian about gentle, temporary supplements. Create a cozy, secure retreat space where they can feel safe. Most animals gradually adjust within weeks to a few months, though their profound bond may mean they always show subtle signs of missing their furry mortal friend.

The decision to introduce a new pet is never a replacement; it is the beginning of a new chapter, and it must be approached with profound care. You must wait until your grieving pet shows stable behavior and an authentic, sustained interest in social interaction. The worst mistake is to rush the process, as this only introduces confusion and intense stress for both your grieving companion and the hopeful newcomer.

There is no universal timeline—some animals benefit quickly from new companionship, easing the void left by their departed furry mortal—while others need an extended period of quiet solitude to complete their healing journey. **Trust your pet to show you the way.**

Becoming Their Fiercest Advocate

Shelby

Shelby - Our Willful Golden Child

"We had recently lost our beloved Lacey J, the daughter of my mom's Sheltie, and decided to adopt a shelter dog. At the SPCA, we saw a tiny fluffball with a blunt nose, soft and sweet. We guessed she was a collie/shepherd mix. She was so relaxed that we worried she might not have much personality, but decided that she was the one for us. Later we found out that she was exhausted, having been passed around a tenants' meeting at The Galleria as an example of Neiman Marcus' wonderful annual window display of the SPCA's adoptable animals.

At eight weeks old, she fit into a child's 12" doll basket. Shelby grew transformer-like, with a long snout, huge rack of razor-sharp teeth, giant paws, long, lanky legs, and a gorgeous flowing coat of auburn, brown and black. At a year old, she would lie stretched out in front of our fireplace and measure 6 feet nose to tail.

She was energetic and loved to chew on anything and everything, especially anything made of wood, including the bottom three feet of the garage when we weren't looking. We constantly sprayed absolutely everything inside and out with bitter apple. Next to wood, I was her favorite chew toy. I thought my arms might be scarred for life.

She was incredibly smart and incredibly willful. None of our usual training techniques were working, so we decided to call in a professional. After 10 minutes, she said, "You need to forget most things you ever knew about training dogs, because this dog is part wolf!" After a few pack-training sessions, Shelby blossomed, she finished teething and my arms finally healed. Still a willful child, she would pretend not to hear my commands. Finally in exasperation, I would make a loud "Ahem!" in parental, throat-clearing "excuse-me-young-lady-what-do-you-think-you're-doing" sound, and she would immediately obey! She was just testing me and testing the limits.

She had an incredible vocabulary, and knew not only the names of all her many toys and other objects, she could comprehend complex instructions. "Shelby, go get the big squeaky toy and take it to Daddy." She would instantly grab the correct toy and run upstairs to drop it at his feet. She was also the most social dog I had ever seen, and absolutely loved people. Everyone was her friend.

One day, a friend called to say they had found a Sheltie in the middle of a lake, near a bridge. They scooped her up into their boat just before she drowned. They asked if we would "foster" her until they found the parent. A few hours later, this thin, scared dog was in our kitchen. She walked over to Shelby's food bowl and started eating. Then she drank from Shelby's water bowl. Shelby stood still and watched. Then the exhausted "Molly" (as in the Unsinkable Molly Brown) climbed into Shelby's giant soft bed. Shelby then laid down on the floor in front of the bed, as if to protect her. We quickly determined she had been abused, and dumped in the lake, and thus Molly joined our pack.

A few years later, we awoke to find Shelby had developed overnight a lump the size of a golf ball on her right front leg. A quick trip to our beloved vet confirmed it was osteosarcoma – bone cancer. After buckets of tears and days of agonizing over whether to amputate or not, we heard of a new clinical trial for canine osteosarcoma. The trial was conducted in conjunction with a private foundation, Texas A&M's veterinary school and MD Anderson, because bone cancer occurs in children as well. The preliminary results were in the MIT Technology Review, "Tiny Drill Attacks Tough Tumors." We eagerly enrolled Shelby, and in the various treatments, she was among the first dogs ever to have a PET scan. The experimental treatments and collaboration would ultimately influence how children and dogs with osteosarcoma were treated. Unfortunately, there is still no cure.

There was an increasing risk that Shelby's weakened bone could break at any time with normal activity. We agonized at the thought it could happen when we weren't home, that she would be in pain and with a broken bone, she would have to be put down immediately. Eventually, we opted to amputate, as dogs respond well to having only three legs, and she became our "tripawd." It didn't really slow her down, but we covered our hardwood floors with carpet remnants so she'd have better traction. She could still run and catch a Frisbee. Now she got to swim in the pool as often as she liked. We no longer cared if she got hair in the drains. She loved the buoyancy. Molly would race around the edges, barking at her to get out.

We would take her back to A&M for occasional tests at the vet school, and she would pull on her leash and stop in front of an office doorway if she saw any vet or technician who had ever worked with her. She had no fear of being there because everyone was her friend, and friends stop by to say hello, of course.

She lived her best life, of unconditional love, laughter, and purpose, until she told us it was time to let her go. Our golden child deserved her rest and her heavenly reward. We took her to our beloved vet, and with her and Shelby's favorite vet tech, together we all tearfully caressed her to say goodbye. As the injection neared her fur, Shelby gave her a kiss.

We are comforted by the certainty that when it is our time to go, she'll be there to greet us."

— Carol & Jim, Shelby's Mom and Dad

What Fierce Looks Like

What happens when our deep love for our pets, combined with a lack of understanding or outdated beliefs, inadvertently leads to suffering? This isn't just a rhetorical question; it's a stark reality that far too many pet parents and their beloved companions have faced. This chapter isn't about looking back at past regrets, but about looking forward, armed with the tools to make truly compassionate choices.

You have the power to transform the end-of-life experience for your pet. This change starts with you becoming the expert on your pet. That means actively learning, using that knowledge, and standing up for your pet's needs.

Here's how you can gain and wield that vital knowledge:

- **Become an Active Participant in Your Pet's Healthcare:** Don't simply defer to veterinary advice. Ask questions. Understand diagnoses, prognoses, and treatment options. If something doesn't make sense, or if you need more information, speak up. Your vet is your partner, but you are your pet's primary advocate.

- **Educate Yourself on Quality-of-Life Assessments:** Learn to objectively evaluate your pet's day-to-day well-being. This goes beyond just eating and drinking. Understand indicators of pain, comfort, joy, and engagement. Many veterinarians use tools like the HHHHHMM scale (Hurt, Hunger, Hydration, Hygiene, Happiness, Mobility, "More good days than bad days") or similar frameworks. Familiarize yourself with these, or create your own system, to track subtle changes. This

171   Furry Mortals

objective data will be there to help guide you when making difficult decisions.

- **Understand the End-of-Life Process:** Knowledge dispels fear. Learn about what to expect as your pet declines, common signs of pain or discomfort, and the various options for comfort care. If euthanasia becomes necessary, understand the procedure step-by-step, including potential physical reactions, so you're not caught off guard. Demand clarity from your veterinary team about every phase.

- **Research Holistic and Supportive Therapies:** Beyond conventional medicine, explore how complementary therapies—like acupuncture, massage, dietary adjustments, or environmental enrichment—can improve comfort and quality of life. This book will guide you through many of these, but your own research, always in consultation with your vet, is invaluable.

- **Communicate Openly and Assertively with Your Veterinary Team:** Share your concerns, your observations about your pet's daily life, and your fears. Don't hesitate to voice your preferences regarding how their final moments, and the aftermath, are handled. If you have specific wishes regarding privacy, post-euthanasia procedures, or the handling of remains, communicate them clearly and in advance.

- **Advocate for Dignified Aftercare:** The care doesn't end with your pet's last breath. Understand the options for cremation or burial and the associated processes. Demand respectful and empathetic treatment from all clinic staff, from the front desk to the technicians handling your pet's remains. Your grief is real, and it deserves to be honored.

This chapter, and indeed this entire book, is a call to action. By actively seeking to understand, by learning to assess genuine quality of life, by openly communicating with veterinarians, and by advocating for dignified care, we can transform the pain of goodbye into a final act of profound love. The goal is clear: to ensure that no pet suffers needlessly, and that no pet parent carries the heavy burden of regret that comes from uninformed decisions or inadequate support.

We can, and we absolutely must, do better for our beloved companions, and for ourselves. This journey is hard, but together, we can make it one of peace, dignity, and profound love.

Open Communication

Although this chapter falls later in the book, it very well may be the most important chapter in the entire book.

Knowing is only half the battle; the other, equally critical half is open communication. It's the bridge that connects your newfound knowledge with your veterinarian's expertise, transforming abstract understanding into actionable, compassionate care for your pet. Without it, even the most well-intentioned efforts can fall short, leaving both you and your pet feeling unheard or underserved.

Think of your veterinarian not just as a medical provider, but as your most vital partner in your pet's end-of-life journey. This partnership thrives on a two-way flow of information. You bring an intimate understanding of your pet's personality, daily habits, subtle changes, and emotional well-being. Your veterinarian brings medical knowledge, diagnostic tools, treatment options, and an understanding of disease progression and pain management. When these two perspectives are candidly shared and integrated, you create the most comprehensive and compassionate care plan possible.

So, how do you foster this essential open communication?

- **Share Your Observations, No Matter How Small:** You are with your pet every day, observing the nuanced shifts that a vet might not catch during a brief clinic visit. Don't dismiss seemingly minor changes in eating habits, sleep patterns, mobility, or even subtle shifts in their gaze or demeanor. Jot them down. Being able to articulate these observations clearly to your vet provides invaluable insights that can help them assess your pet's true quality of life and progression of illness.

Be specific: "She used to jump onto the couch easily, now she hesitates and sometimes needs help," or "His breathing seems heavier after just a short walk."

- **Ask Every Question, Even the *Silly Ones*:** There's no such thing as a foolish question when it comes to your pet's comfort and your peace of mind. If you don't understand a diagnosis, a treatment plan, or a prognosis, ask for clarification. If you're concerned about pain management, medication side effects, or potential future scenarios, voice those concerns. Inquire about what to expect during decline, potential emergencies, or the specifics of the euthanasia process if that conversation becomes necessary. Knowing what to anticipate reduces anxiety.

- **Clearly State Your Goals and Priorities:** Your veterinarian needs to understand what matters most to *you* and your pet in their final chapter. Is your absolute priority pain relief? Maintaining a certain level of mobility? Avoiding clinic visits as much as possible? Or are you willing to pursue aggressive treatment if there's a strong chance of extending truly good quality life? Articulate your priorities clearly. This helps your vet tailor recommendations that align with your values, rather than simply offering every possible medical intervention without considering your specific context.

- **Discuss the "What Ifs" and Plan Ahead:** It's uncomfortable, but necessary, to talk about the "what if" scenarios. What if your pet suddenly declines over a weekend? What if they stop eating entirely? What if their pain becomes unmanageable at home? Discussing these possibilities *before* they happen allows you to create a proactive plan with your vet, preventing panicked, rushed decisions in moments of crisis. This includes talking openly about euthanasia long before it becomes an immediate necessity, understanding the process, and making arrangements for location and aftercare.

- **Advocate for Your Pet's Dignity and Your Own Peace:** If a procedure or conversation makes you uncomfortable, or if you feel a lack of empathy, express it. If you have specific wishes for your pet's final moments—such as wanting privacy, a particular environment, or time to grieve afterward, communicate these desires clearly. A truly compassionate veterinary team will respect and facilitate these needs. If you encounter resistance or insensitivity, don't be afraid to seek another opinion or another practice; your peace of mind during this tender time is paramount.

Open communication isn't just about exchanging facts; it's about building a trusting relationship with your veterinary team based on mutual respect and shared goals. **It allows you to become a powerful, informed advocate for your pet, ensuring their final days are filled with the dignity, comfort, and love they so profoundly deserve.**

Talking With Your Vet

When you are under the emotional strain of the "In-Between," it is easy to feel overwhelmed by medical jargon or the rush of a busy clinic. Use these prompts to ensure your voice—and your pet's needs—are the primary focus of the conversation.

1. Lead with Quality of Life, Not Just Data

Instead of asking, "What do the blood results say?" try:

"She is struggling at home. How can we adjust her care to bring back her spark, or is this the limit of what medicine can do?"

2. Ask the "Gawande" Questions

To find the right path, ask your vet these three clarifying questions:

"What is the best-case scenario if we do this treatment, and what is the most likely scenario for his comfort?"

"What does 'success' look like for this procedure? Does it mean more time, or does it mean better quality?"

"If this were your own 'furry mortal,' knowing what you know, what would you do right now?"

3. Define Your "Red Lines"

Be clear about what you are willing to put your pet through.

"My goal is to avoid an emergency crisis at midnight. Can we create a plan that prioritizes a peaceful passing, even if it means doing it sooner than medically necessary?"

4. The Logistics of the Threshold

If you are considering euthanasia, ask the practical questions now so you don't have to think about them during the event:

"Do you offer home visits, or is there a quiet room at the clinic?"

"What are the specific steps? Will there be a sedative first to help them sleep?"

"Can I stay with them the entire time?"

Reminder

You are the world's leading expert on your pet.

The vet knows the disease; you know the soul. If the medical plan feels like it is fighting the body but losing the spirit, you have the right to say no. Choosing comfort over cure is not giving up—it is the ultimate act of fierce advocacy.

Prioritizing Dignity and Peace

As pet parents, our greatest gift to our companions is not just the love we shower on them throughout their lives, but also the peace and dignity we can ensure in their final moments. This isn't about prolonging life at all costs, but about recognizing when the balance shifts, and comfort, respect, and freedom from suffering become the paramount goals. Prioritizing dignity and peace means making choices that honor your pet's entire life, ensuring their final chapter is as gentle and loving as possible. This philosophy rests on several key pillars:

- **Understand What Dignity and Peace Look Like for Your Pet:** Dignity and peace aren't one-size-fits-all concepts. For a playful dog, it might mean the ability to still enjoy short, gentle walks outside without pain. For a cat, it could be the quiet comfort of a favorite sunbeam, free from nausea or labored breathing. Take time to truly observe your pet. What activities still bring them joy? What actions now cause them distress? Dignity means they can still engage in aspects of life that define them, even if on a smaller scale. Peace means the absence of preventable suffering, both physical and emotional.

- **Pain Management is Paramount:** A pet cannot have dignity or peace if they are in pain. This extends beyond obvious limping or vocalizations. Subtle signs like reluctance to move, changes in eating habits, restlessness, or increased irritability can all indicate discomfort. Work closely with your veterinarian to establish an effective pain management plan. This might involve oral medications, injectables, or even alternative therapies. Be vigilant and proactive in assessing and addressing any signs of pain. It is your right, and your pet's right, to live free from unnecessary suffering.

- **Choose Quality Over Quantity:** This is often the hardest shift in mindset. Our natural inclination is to want more time with our beloved pets. However, truly compassionate care means understanding when more time equals more suffering. When aggressive treatments offer little chance of true recovery or significantly diminish quality of life, prioritizing dignity means focusing on comfort care. This could mean opting for comfort measures rather than curative ones or making the difficult decision for euthanasia before suffering becomes overwhelming. Reflect on what a "good day" truly means for your pet, and if those good days are becoming increasingly rare.

- **Create a Sacred Space for Their Final Days:** If your pet is declining at home, dedicate efforts to making their environment as comfortable and peaceful as possible. This might involve soft bedding, easy access to food, water, and litter boxes, non-slip surfaces for unsteady pets, and a quiet, calm atmosphere. Minimize loud noises, sudden movements, or anything that might cause them stress. Your home can become a true sanctuary for their final moments, filled with love and warmth.

- **Honor Their Legacy Through a Peaceful Passing:** Whether through a natural passing or euthanasia, the final moments are sacred. If euthanasia is chosen, prioritize a calm, compassionate experience. This might mean an at-home euthanasia, or a quiet room at the clinic. Be present, hold them, speak comforting words. Ensure the process is explained to you fully beforehand, and that your wishes for privacy and aftercare are respected.

Prioritizing dignity and peace in your pet's end-of-life journey is one of the most profound expressions of love you can offer. It requires courage, honesty, and a willingness to put their well-being above your own desire for their continued presence. But in doing so, **you ensure their final moments are filled with the comfort and respect they so deeply deserve**, leaving you with a sense of profound peace amidst your grief.

The Fierce Advocate: The Sacred Stewardship of the Threshold

To love a furry mortal is to eventually be called to a higher duty. In the beginning, your role was simple: provider, playmate, and protector. But as the muzzle silvers and the pace slows, your role undergoes a profound transformation. You are no longer just a pet parent; you have become the **Fierce Advocate**.

Being a fierce advocate is the most courageous form of love. It is the commitment to stand in the "In-Between"—that liminal space where medicine reaches its limits and the soul begins its departure—and refuse to look away.

The Advocate's Creed

The fierce advocate understands that while the veterinarian is the expert on the **disease**, they are the world's leading expert on the **soul**. Your advocacy is built on three pillars:

- **Mercy Over Longevity:** The world will tell you to fight for every second. The Advocate asks, *"What is the quality of those seconds?"* You prioritize a peaceful "now" over a painful "later," recognizing that a week of comfort is worth more than a month of medical intervention that strips away dignity.

- **The Voice for the Silent:** Animals do not complain; they simply endure. Advocacy means learning the "Natural Language of Departure"—the subtle shift in breath, the glassy gaze, the withdrawal into a "den." You speak the words they cannot, telling the clinical world when "enough is enough."

- **Persistent Grace:** You carry the emotional weight so they don't have to. When you choose euthanasia or a quiet home-hospice transition, you are essentially taking the physical suffering of the animal and transforming it into the emotional grief of the human. This is the ultimate act of selflessness.

The Shield of Dignity

As an advocate, you act as a shield between your pet and the medicalized fog. You ask the hard questions: Is this for them, or is it for me? Will this treatment return them to their 'Top Three' joys, or just keep their heart beating?

When you embrace this role, the "Hardest Walk" ceases to be a tragedy of loss and becomes a masterpiece of stewardship. You are the gatekeeper. You ensure that their final memories are not of sterile tables and cold needles, but of your scent, your steady hand, and the vibration of your voice whispering their sweet, necessary name.

To be a Fierce Advocate is to honor the unconditional legacy. You are the guardian of their story, ensuring that the final chapter is written with the same tenderness and respect that defined the first. You did not fail them by letting go; you fulfilled your most sacred promise. You walked them home.

The Emergency Advocate

Finding Clarity in the Crisis

When a diagnosis is sudden, time seems to vanish, your brain will go into survival mode. You will feel pressured, panicked, and overwhelmed by x-rays, charts and clinical jargon. Now is the time to slow the world down for just a few minutes so you can be there for your furry mortal.

1. Breathe and Pause

Unless your pet is in active, gasping respiratory distress that requires immediate intervention, you usually have ten minutes.

- **Ask the Vet:** "Can I have a few quiet minutes alone with [Pet's Name] to process this before we make a final decision?"
- **The Purpose:** This breaks the conveyor belt feeling of the ER and allows you to reconnect with your furry mortal, not just the symptoms.

2. The Three Critical Questions

For clarity ask your care team these specific questions:

- **The Comfort Question:** "If we pursue treatment today, what is the *immediate* impact on their comfort level?"
- **The "Identity" Question:** "Will the recovery process from this intervention allow them to return to their **joy markers**, or are we just maintaining biological function?"

- **The Professional Perspective:** "If this were your pet, and you knew their personality like I do, would you feel like today is the day to protect their dignity?"

3. The Gut-Check

You don't have time for a worksheet, so look at your pet right now.

- Is the "spark" that makes them *them* still visible through the pain?
- If the cancer or trauma has already claimed two of their three pillars (their voice, their greeting, their presence), then the choice you make now isn't a betrayal—it's a rescue.

4. I Am Here, I Am Your Voice

The hardest part of a crisis is the feeling that you are "quitting" too soon. Remind yourself again: "I am not ending their life; I am ending their suffering. My readiness to say goodbye is not a requirement for their need to go."

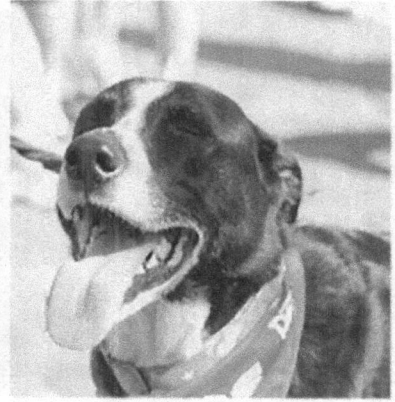

Besties!

furry mortal

[noun]

A bright, furry presence whose physical time is a gift of pure light, proving that even a short stay on earth can leave a permanent, glowing thumbprint on the human heart.

Embracing the Future

Dutchy

Dutchy - I Trusted He Knew What Was Best for Me

"I was working in a small town and had just purchased a house. A few weeks after I moved in, two small dogs were making their way across the street. They were thin and dirty. I took them in and found a home for the little girl but I knew the little boy needed to be with me. I named him Dutchy. He was losing the use of his back legs and didn't want to eat. After a few thousand dollars of vet visits, x-rays, and blood tests, there was no answer. I took him to a vet in another town who was able to treat and cure my baby boy. I was advised that he would not live as long as I wanted him to because the medications would cause problems for him in his later years. I put that information in the back of my brain and he and I decided we would get through it together and do whatever it took for him to have a wonderful life.

He started to grow and gain weight. His red coat got thicker and his small legs got stronger. He started to run and play and was by my side every minute I wasn't at work. **Dutchy was my protector and my best friend.**

We moved to Houston where he excelled and everyone that met him fell in love with him. After a few years in an apartment, we bought a house and everyone in the neighborhood helped take care of him when I had to travel. He was the glue that kept my life together and I came to realize I didn't save him because he saved me. He got me through a hurricane, the loss of my mom, a mugging, and some of the worst times of my life.

And then the day came where the cancer couldn't be kept at bay. He was tired, his eyes were not as bright, and I was getting the look from him that was saying "Mom, it's time and you need to let go!" I realized the best gift I could give him was to let him go. Along our journey, he had been given a sister name Tallulah. She looked just like him but taller and longer. He knew she would be there for me and that I would be taken care of. He knew the 11 years we spent together would be the best of my life. He knew I loved him more than anything on earth and that I trusted him to know what was best for me.

And then on December 21, 2011, my first grandson was born. I took Dutchy to the vet and she and Dutchy let me know it was time for him to get his rest. So on Christmas Eve, my son came home and we took Dutchy so he could cross to the Rainbow Bridge. The vet told me he had never seen a dog look at his parent the way Dutchy looked at me. He knew there was something special between the two of us and I told him about our 11 years together.

As he closed Dutch's eyes, he let me kiss his nose one last time and then he prepared his box for burial. I felt at peace and I knew that feisty, sweet, loving boy that I had taken in 11 years earlier was what possibly saved my life. He and I are forever bonded and there are still days that I break down and cry for him. It was that love and that bond that allowed me to be ok after letting him go. There are times that I still walk into a room and feel him there. He will forever be in my life and I know I did the right thing.

Letting your pet go is a special, caring, and precious way to let them know what they meant to you. And for Dutchy and I, he is forever my soul dog."

— Cheryl, Dutchy's Mom

Future of Goodbyes

The landscape of pet end-of-life care is evolving, driven by a deeper understanding of the human-animal bond and a growing demand for more compassionate, personalized options.

No longer confined to traditional veterinary clinic settings, saying goodbye to a beloved pet can now encompass a range of choices designed to prioritize comfort, dignity, and a truly meaningful farewell. These new trends offer solace and support, helping pet parents navigate one of life's most challenging passages.

One of the most significant shifts is the rise of specialized facilities dedicated to peaceful euthanasia. They offer a serene, compassionate environment where you can bring your pet for their final moments. These facilities are designed to be calm and comforting, minimizing the stress often associated with a traditional veterinary office. They provide private rooms and dedicated staff focused solely on making the goodbye as gentle as possible, offering a tranquil alternative to the often-bustling general clinic setting.

Beyond the immediate moment of passing, new trends are emerging in how we honor our pets' physical forms and memories. Pet water cremation, also known as aquamation or alkaline hydrolysis, is gaining popularity as an environmentally friendlier alternative to traditional flame-based cremation. This gentle process uses water and an alkali solution to break down the body, resulting in a sterile liquid and bone fragments that are then processed into ashes. Many pet parents find this method to be a more peaceful and respectful option, aligning with a desire for a greener goodbye.

The desire to keep our pets' memories close has also led to a burgeoning industry of pet memorial keepsakes. Beyond traditional urns, families can now choose from a vast array of personalized tributes. This might include custom jewelry infused with a tiny amount of ashes, paw print molds transformed into decorative art, portraits painted from photographs, or even unique glass art incorporating cremains. These keepsakes offer tangible comfort, allowing cherished memories to be physically present in our daily lives.

There's a growing recognition of the importance of early intervention and long-term health, particularly in areas like pet cancer. By raising awareness and supporting research into early diagnostic methods, such initiatives aim to give pets a better chance at successful treatment and extended quality of life, potentially postponing the need for end-of-life decisions. This proactive approach to health complements compassionate end-of-life care by striving to maximize healthy years.

These new trends reflect a collective evolution in how we view our pets – not just as animals, but as beloved family members whose passing deserves as much consideration, compassion, and personalization as any other significant loss. By embracing these options, we can ensure that our final act of love truly honors the unique bond we share, providing comfort not only to our pets but also to our grieving hearts.

Sustainable Tributes

When the time comes for the final goodbye, our love for our pets drives us to look beyond the ordinary, seeking personalized and meaningful ways to honor their lives that align with our values. This has led to the emergence of truly innovative and sustainable farewell options.

Sustainable and Gentle Disposition

The choice of disposition is increasingly moving toward eco-friendly methods that are seen as more respectful and gentle. Aquamation (water cremation) is a beautiful and significant development that uses water over traditional flame cremation. It is often preferred for its significantly lower environmental impact, and the resulting sterile bone fragments are often lighter and finer. For those who feel a deep connection to the earth, natural burial on one's own land can be a profoundly comforting option, turning a piece of property into sacred ground (though you must always consult local laws first).

New Ways to Cherish Their Memory

We crave tangible ways to keep our furry mortals close, and modern advancements offer heartfelt possibilities that provide alternatives to conventional ash. If you want something more tangible than loose ashes, services like **Parting Stone** (see Furry Mortal Resources) can transform cremated remains into a collection of 5–40 clean, smooth, naturally varying "stones". These solidified remains are entirely made of the pet's remains, offering a comforting object you can hold, display, or carry with you. You can then even place a stone in their favorite places as a memorial to the memories you made together.

Through memorial art and jewelry, artisans can integrate a tiny portion of the ashes into glass art, resin pieces, or precious metal jewelry, transforming the remains into stunning, lasting tributes. Alternatively, carbon extracted from the remains can be used to create memorial diamonds, or a small amount of ash can even be mixed into tattoo ink for an intimate, permanent memorial. For those who seek a lasting art piece for the home, companies design and sell handcrafted, artisan pet urns and memorials—primarily ceramic and wooden—that function as beautiful, respectful decor.

Living Tributes and Lasting Legacies

For those who desire their pet's memory to contribute to new life, there are options for creating peaceful, living memorials and sustainable legacies. Through memorial gardens and forests, a simple choice is to scatter your pet's ashes in a favorite garden or special spot. Services like memorial forests (e.g., **Better Place Forests**, see Furry Mortal Resources) offer a shared and protected final resting place where your pet's ashes can be spread at the base of a memorial tree, turning their final resting place into a beautiful, enduring tribute. And, when the time comes, your ashes can be placed at the same memorial tree. A loving, living tribute to the great bond you shared.

Concepts like renewal pods or eco-friendly urns made of beeswax allow you to place remains or ashes within a biodegradable container designed to nourish the growth of a tree or plant, powerfully symbolizing new life and renewal emerging from loss.

These evolving trends speak volumes about the deep, unconditional bond we share. They offer us more compassionate and personalized ways to say goodbye, allowing us to **choose a farewell that aligns with our deepest values and provides comfort during a profoundly difficult time**.

Managing Your Pet's Social Media Legacy

In our modern world, a pet's life is often documented in real-time through dedicated Instagram accounts, TikToks, and Facebook pages. **Oliver had more followers on social media than I ever will!** When a furry mortal passes, their digital presence remains, often serving as a vibrant, living archive of their spirit. Deciding how to manage this digital legacy is a deeply personal step in the grieving process. For many, these accounts transition from a place of daily updates to a digital memorial—a memory anchor in the cloud where the community that loved your pet can gather to share their own stories and collective grief.

When you are ready, consider which path feels most aligned with your heart:

The Living Archive (The "Legacy" Account)

Many pet parents choose to leave the account active but transition it into a memorial. You might post a final, beautiful tribute—perhaps a photo collage or a heartfelt message—and then "pin" that post to the top of the profile. This allows the page to exist as a permanent gallery of joy where you and others can return to revisit favorite memories without the pressure of creating new content.

The Final Farewell

If maintaining the account feels like an emotional burden it is perfectly okay to close it. Before doing so, most platforms allow you to download a complete archive of your data. Securing these photos and videos first ensures that while the public-facing account is gone, your private library of memories is safe. You can then post a final sign-off, thanking everyone for their support, before deactivating the page.

Transitioning to Advocacy

Some find healing by evolving the account into a platform for a cause. A page once dedicated to a single pet can become a voice for senior dog adoption, breed-specific rescue, or support for others navigating this journey. This turns your pet's digital footprint into a "Living Celebration," allowing their impact to continue helping other furry mortals long after they have moved on.

Regardless of what you choose, remember that you are the keeper of your pet's story, both offline and online. There is no right or wrong way to handle a digital goodbye; there is only the way that brings you the most peace.

Grief in the Digital Neighborhood

For much of history, the death of a furry mortal was a solitary experience. You mourned within the four walls of your home and perhaps received a polite but brief nod of sympathy from a neighbor. But the digital age has fundamentally rewritten the geography of grief. Today, when the sudden quiet of a vacant home becomes too loud to bear at 3:00 AM, you no longer have to sit in the dark alone. The internet has given us a virtual tribe a global, 24-hour sanctuary where the heartbreak of losing a pet is not just understood but honored as a significant life event.

In this digital neighborhood, the disenfranchised nature of pet loss begins to dissolve. Online forums, social media support groups, and moderated communities like the **Association for Pet Loss and Bereavement (APLB)** provide a space for what I call anonymous empathy. There is a unique, raw honesty that flourishes when you are surrounded by strangers who are all speaking the same language of loss. In these spaces, you don't have to worry about being too much or staying sad for too long. You can share the specific, singular ways your pet used to talk or the guilt you feel over a medical decision, and you will find a chorus of voices saying, *"I hear you. I've been there. Your feelings are valid."*

While a virtual tribe can be a powerful bridge to healing, it can also be a double-edged sword. Grief is highly personal, and sometimes, seeing a constant stream of other people's trauma can inadvertently add weight to your own. To ensure your online experience remains a source of strength rather than a drain on your energy, it is important to engage with intention. As you look for your own virtual tribe, use the following guide to help you navigate these communities with grace and self-protection.

Best Practices for Engaging in Online Support Groups

- **Lurk Before You Leap:** Before posting your own story, spend some time reading through the threads. This allows you to understand the group's culture, the tone of the conversations, and whether the moderators are active in keeping the space safe.

- **Guard Your Privacy:** While vulnerability is a key to healing, remember that these are public or semi-public spaces. Use a first name or a pseudonym and avoid sharing sensitive personal details like your home address or specific financial information.

- **Set Emotional Boundaries:** It is okay to step away. If the stories of others become too heavy or trigger your own anticipatory grief too intensely, give yourself permission to close the tab. You are there to heal, not to carry the weight of the entire world.

- **Be the Support You Seek:** Empathy is a two-way street. Often, the most profound healing comes from offering a kind word to someone else who is just starting their journey. By validating another's pain, you subconsciously validate your own.

- **Verify the Gatekeepers:** Look for groups that have clear rules and active moderators. A well-moderated group prevents trolling and ensures that the environment remains respectful and focused on support.

- **Keep Your Expectations Realistic:** Online groups are wonderful for emotional validation and shared experience, but they are not a substitute for professional mental health care or medical advice. If your grief feels unmanageable or stuck, seek out a professional counselor who specializes in the human-animal bond.

Pet Loss as a Recognized Human Right

For too long, the grief associated with the death of a furry mortal has been relegated to the shadows of disenfranchised grief. This is a term used by sociologists to describe a loss that society doesn't fully acknowledge, validate, or provide space for. It is the sting of a boss asking why you're distracted a day after losing your best friend, or a friend or family member saying, "*It's okay, you can just get another one.*" But the future of pet end-of-life care isn't just about better medicine or digital support; it is about a fundamental shift in our cultural DNA. We are moving toward a world where the bond between a human and an animal is recognized as a profound, legally and socially protected human right.

This shift is already beginning to manifest in our laws and corporate structures. We are seeing the rise of "paw-ternity" or pet bereavement leave, where companies acknowledge that the loss of a companion animal requires the same emotional processing time as the loss of a human family member. In the future, this will not be a perk offered by progressive startups, but a standard labor expectation. When we recognize that the caregiving burden and the subsequent mourning are significant life events, we dismantle the shame and isolation that so often haunt the pet parent's journey.

Furthermore, the physical landscape of our cities is changing to accommodate this narrative. The future holds the development of specialized pet hospices—stand-alone facilities designed not for surgery or cures, but for the sacred work of transition. These spaces will be designed like homes, offering families the ability to stay overnight with their pets, surrounded by gardens and peace, away from the clinical antiseptic smell of a traditional hospital. This societal investment in dying well for animals reflects our own evolving humanity.

As we shift this narrative, we also change the way we support the veterinary professionals who stand on the front lines. A culture that validates pet loss is a culture that protects its vets from burnout and compassion fatigue. When society recognizes the weight of the work being done, we provide better resources for those who facilitate these final goodbyes. We move toward a multi-disciplinary approach where every clinic has access to a grief counselor, ensuring the hand to hold is always available.

Ultimately, recognizing pet loss as a human right is about honoring the truth of our hearts. It is a collective agreement that love is not limited by species, and therefore, grief should not be limited by societal awkwardness. By demanding space for our sorrow, we ensure that the legacy of our furry mortals is one of dignity. **We are building a future where no one must hide their tears behind a desk or apologize for the size of the hole left in their life.**

The Rise of Veterinary Social Work

For decades, the veterinary clinic has been a place of high-stakes science and technical precision. But as any pet parent who has sat in a quiet exam room knows, the medical diagnosis is only half the story. The other half is human: the crushing weight of a decision, the financial anxiety, and the profound grief that begins long before the final breath is taken. The future of end-of-life care recognizes that a pet's doctor cannot be expected to manage the complex emotional ecosystem of the human family alone. This is where the rise of **Veterinary Social Work (VSW)** is fundamentally changing the landscape of care.

Veterinary Social Work is an emerging multi-disciplinary field that bridges the gap between the stethoscope and the soul. In the clinics of the future, a fierce advocate won't just be interacting with a veterinarian and a technician; they will be supported by a trained social worker who specializes in the human-animal bond. This professional's role is not to treat the pet, but to "treat" the bond. They are there to facilitate difficult family meetings, help owners navigate the medical paradox of choice, and provide immediate crisis intervention during the trauma of an emergency.

The presence of a social worker allows for a wrap-around care model. While the veterinarian focuses on pharmaceutical pain management or genomic insights, the social worker focuses on the caregiver's burden. They help the family assess their own limitations, validate their feelings of guilt, and provide a shoulder to lean on that isn't rushed by the demands of the next surgical appointment. This model acknowledges a truth we have long ignored: the mental health of the human is inextricably linked to the quality of life of the pet. If a pet parent is paralyzed by grief or overwhelmed by the daily routine of care, the pet's experience suffers as well.

This future model protects our furry mortals by protecting the veterinary team itself. By delegating the intense emotional labor to a social work professional, veterinarians are freed to focus on their clinical expertise without the heavy toll of emotional fatigue. This reduces burnout and ensures that the entire clinic environment remains a sanctuary of calm rather than a pressure cooker of unaddressed sorrow.

As we look forward, the standard of best care will no longer be measured solely by the sophistication of the medical equipment, but by the depth of the emotional support available. We are moving toward a future where no pet parent has to navigate the mortgage of the heart in a vacuum. By integrating social work into the heart of the clinic, we ensure that the final journey is a shared one, supported by a team that honors both the animal's life and the human's love with equal reverence.

Oliver

A Call to Collective Action

Riley

Riley - The Unsinkable Riley J.

"To meet Riley is to meet a force of nature condensed into a tiny, fiery package. **At an astonishing 23 1/2 years old, Riley is a living legend, a tiny tortie with the strength of a lioness.** She celebrated her 21st birthday with a party complete with bottles of "Purr"secco (what else do you do when you hit the legal drinking age???). Her 22nd birthday was celebrated with a Taylor Swift "22" party and her 23rd was a Taco Cat party with all her favorite people. Every birthday party brought with it the apprehension that this could be her last ... but still she persists! She's outlasted three of her siblings and a whole roster of cousins, a quiet testament to her indomitable spirit.

Riley's longevity is not without its concessions to time. She walks much slower (unless you are trying to give her daily pills) and with much more purpose. Her appetite, always a delicate affair, has become so particular that she is arguably the pickiest eater in the world, demanding a constant, rotating menu of acceptable flavors and textures. Twice a week, she undergoes subcutaneous fluid therapy, a routine her veterinary team in Texas uses to keep her hydrated, and she's on a cocktail of daily medications. Anyone looking at her medical chart would see the undeniable markers of extreme age.

But a veterinary chart, much like a mere list of years, only tells part of the story. The true measure of Riley's life, the one that matters most to her devoted mom, Jill, is her quality of life assessment. And on this score, the tiny tortie remains spectacularly, unequivocally thriving.

The assessment of an elderly pet's well-being relies not on medical statistics alone, but on core behaviors—the things that make them. For Riley, this includes the daily ritual of "giving you the business." Her feisty personality is fully intact. She might move slower, but her mind is sharp, and her attitude is sharper. When she wants something like to be brushed, or wonders where you are, she communicates her needs with a very authoritative "meowr".

She finds joy in the simple, yet profound, pleasures: the perfect sunbeam on her favorite bed, a quiet perch by a familiar window, and the warm, deep purr that still vibrates with happiness when lays on Jill's chest … keeping Jill pinned on the sofa for hours, because we all know you don't move when the cat is happy. She still engages, still connects, and still, most importantly, feels secure and loved at home.

Riley's life is a masterclass in adaptation. She needs steps to get up on the furniture, her weekly fluids are a must, she still runs from taking her pills (but easier to catch these days), and she will refuse to eat the salmon primavera she loved last week, but none of these necessary accommodations have dulled the inner light that makes her Riley.

She's not just surviving; she is thriving—a happy, sassy, feline firecracker."

— Angela, Riley's Aunt

An Update I Did Not Want to Make

I struggled with the thought of adding this paragraph, as my wish was to share Riley's story while she was still with us. But on New Year's Eve, Riley began her next journey. Though she was no longer able to walk on her own, her final hours were filled with dignity, comfort, and an abundance of treats. I went over to Jill's house to spend that quiet, early morning at home with them. We brushed her coat and let her rest on the blankets she loved most. She even enjoyed one last feast of her favorite cheese, eating like a true champ until the end. **Riley crossed the rainbow bridge quietly lying in her mom's lap in her own home surrounded by love.**

Since she has gone, the silence in Jill's home is heavy; it is a quietness no one is used to, missing the sound of Riley paws, her cantankerous meows and the energy she brought to every room. Riley was a soul loved by many and will be missed by just as many. As she joins her siblings who went before her, I have no doubt she is already back to keeping them all on their toes just like the Riley we will always remember.

Finding Your Village

I think it's important to look beyond just that immediate, painful moment of saying goodbye. **My primary focus is on a powerful movement dedicated to enhancing the quality of life for pets who are battling a serious or terminal illness.** Providing vital support to their devoted parents through that incredibly challenging time is just as important to me. I've watched this effort grow, driven by significant advances in comfort and hospice care and the impactful work done by specialized non-profit organizations.

These groups are truly at the forefront of improving our pets' final chapters. They provide research, valuable education, and direct assistance, often focusing on specific areas of pet health, like early disease detection, or offering comprehensive resources specifically for end-of-life care.

Focusing on Longevity Through Early Detection

One significant area of focus for dedicated organizations is early disease detection. The core mission of several key groups is to give parents more precious time with their companions. They do this by passionately raising awareness, educating pet parents about the subtle warning signs of serious pet illnesses, and funding critical research that leads to earlier and more accurate diagnoses.

My own experience with Oliver, my sweet boy who had undiagnosed, metastasized bone cancer, is why I care about this stuff so much. Since we didn't catch his illness early (and we had the chance to as you will see below), his final goodbye felt much more shocking and painful than it should have.

A couple of years before Oliver's final goodbye, our vet found a two-pound mass in his spleen, prompting us to schedule surgery for its removal. While we waited for the surgery date, he had a violent bloody nose. I mean, for those of you who know me, I love the show *Dexter*, and Dexter would have loved my office! Blood was everywhere as he sneezed and sneezed. This bloody nose moved up his surgery because now cancer was likely the culprit for both the mass and the nosebleed.

Oliver had a splenectomy for the large mass and a nasal scan to ensure no masses were in his nasal cavities. We were ecstatic to be told: *"No cancer was found."* We felt so blessed and lucky, as masses like that are usually not benign. But that joy, although we made every minute of it as meaningful as possible, was short-lived. Less than two years later, the devastating truth was revealed: cancer had spread aggressively to his lungs to the point where there wasn't much space for him to breathe. I couldn't process that information, standing there in shock, as I just kept hearing that prior verdict ringing in my ears: "no cancer was found."

The shock of his abrupt passing, coupled with the profound lack of empathy during his final moments, ignited a fierce determination within me. This experience—the trauma of his quick decline and the handling of his remains—solidified my resolve to write this book: for Oliver, my Bubba, and for all pet parents navigating this difficult journey. My search for anything to cling to that could help me process this intense loss.

Enter Moose's March (see Furry Mortal Resources). They are committed to the early detection of pet cancer, aiming for better outcomes and an extended quality of life for beloved companions. They recognize that cancer is a leading cause of death in dogs, but early detection saves lives.

They urge parents to stay vigilant: if a dog shows signs like unusual lumps or bumps, unexplained weight loss, persistent limping, bleeding, or sudden changes in behavior, they must talk to their veterinarian immediately. Catching cancer early increases the chance for treatment, time, and creating more memories together. They connect pet parents with the accessible information and tools needed for early detection and treatment options, working to extend healthy life and giving parents more time to make tough decisions. They are **Marching for More Memories**.

Broader End-of-Life and Bereavement Support

Other organizations also contribute immensely to the broader landscape of pet health and support. The **International Association for Animal Hospice and Comfort Care (IAAHPC)** stands out as a leading resource for both veterinary professionals and pet parents seeking guidance. They not only offer certifications for veterinary professionals but also provide invaluable resources for families navigating these difficult waters.

Numerous pet loss and bereavement support groups, both local and online, offer much-needed emotional support and create a safe space for grieving pet parents to share their experiences and feelings without judgment. One such resource is the Furry Mortals Online Support Group. This community is specifically dedicated to encouraging pet parents to share their personal stories about their pet's final chapter. By openly sharing these experiences, the group helps other pet parents realize they are not alone in their grief or in the complex decisions surrounding their pet's end of life, fostering a sense of collective comfort, and understanding.

And let us not forget the vital contributions of veterinary schools and research institutions. Many universities are actively engaged in groundbreaking research to improve pain management, develop new treatments for age-related diseases, and advance our overall understanding of animal welfare at the end of life.

Finding and Utilizing Resources

When it comes to finding and utilizing these valuable resources, your veterinarian is always a great place to start. They can often recommend local hospice or comfort care specialists and direct you to relevant support organizations. Beyond that, a simple online search using keywords like "pet cancer early detection," "pet hospice [your city]," "pet comfort care," or "pet loss support groups" can help you discover resources in your area or online. Visiting the websites of non-profit organizations or the IAAHPC can also provide a wealth of educational materials, directories of certified professionals, and links to other valuable resources.

By embracing these advancements and actively seeking out the support offered by these dedicated organizations, pet parents can truly ensure their beloved companions receive the most compassionate and comprehensive care possible throughout their lives, right up to their very last moments. **It is about making the best decisions for our cherished family members, ensuring their dignity and comfort are paramount.**

Raising the Standard

The stories I chose to share throughout this book have been deeply personal, often raw, and at times, heartbreaking. They illustrate the profound challenges and the emotional toll that comes with saying goodbye to our beloved animal companions. Yet, within every struggle and every lesson learned, there pulses a powerful message of hope for the future of pet end-of-life care. This hope isn't a passive wish; it's an active call for us, as pet parents, to become the architects of a more compassionate and dignified future for our furry mortals.

The landscape of veterinary medicine is rapidly evolving, and **pet parents are the undeniable catalyst** pushing for transformative change in how end-of-life care is approached.

Our ever-deepening understanding of the human-animal bond, coupled with our growing demand for care that truly honors our pets' final journey, is driving this significant shift. We are collectively moving beyond a reactive, purely medicalized approach to one that prioritizes quality of life, emotional well-being, and environmental comfort above all else. This collective voice guides us to make choices rooted in profound love, rather than fear or a simple desire for longevity at any cost.

So, how can we, as pet parents, continue to actively shape this hopeful future?

1. **Embrace Knowledge as Your Greatest Tool** The most powerful action you can take is to educate yourself. Understand the signs of decline, learn how to assess your pet's quality of life objectively, and familiarize yourself with comfort care options. Knowledge replaces fear with

confidence, allowing you to make proactive, thoughtful decisions rather than reactive, desperate ones. Equip yourself with the information to ask the right questions, understand the answers, and advocate effectively for your pet's needs.

2. **Cultivate Open Communication with Your Care Team** Your care team (including your veterinarian) is your invaluable ally on this journey. Foster a relationship built on trust and transparent dialogue. Share your observations, your concerns, and your ultimate goals for your pet's comfort and dignity. Do not hesitate to ask for detailed explanations, discuss "what-if" scenarios, and clearly articulate your wishes for their final moments. This collaborative approach ensures that your pet's care plan is truly tailored to their individual needs and your family's values.

3. **Prioritize Dignity and Peace Above All Else** This means making choices that reduce suffering and enhance comfort, even if it means letting go sooner than you might wish. It involves vigilant pain management, creating a comfortable home sanctuary, and choosing a passing that is as peaceful and stress-free as possible. Whether through natural progression or euthanasia, focus on ensuring their final experience is one of calm, love, and respect. This selfless act is the ultimate expression of your devotion.

4. **Advocate for Better Standards** Your experiences, positive and negative, matter. Share your feedback with veterinary clinics, funeral services, and even pet product companies. Praise practices that excel in compassionate care, and respectfully voice concerns where improvements are needed, particularly regarding sensitivity in the aftermath of loss. By doing so, you contribute to raising the bar for the entire industry, ensuring that every pet and every family receives the empathy and dignity they deserve.

The journey of saying goodbye to a beloved pet is never easy, but the future is brighter. By embracing knowledge, fostering open communication, prioritizing dignity and peace, and advocating for higher standards, we can transform this most difficult passage into a final, profound act of love. **This is our commitment to our furry mortals, ensuring their last moments on Earth are as cherished and respected as every day that came before.**

The Heartfelt Farewell: Why I Choose to Be There

Saying goodbye to a beloved pet is one of the most agonizing experiences a pet parent faces. It's a decision steeped in love, compassion, and often, profound grief. **For me, when that difficult choice has to be made, there's only one place I can be: right there with them, holding them close as they embark on their final journey.** I have had to say goodbye to six of my own cherished companions and have supported numerous friends through their goodbyes as well, and each time, the importance of being present has been unwavering for me.

For me, being there means offering a final act of love and comfort. It's about providing a familiar touch, a soothing voice, and the reassuring presence of someone who loves them unconditionally in their last moments. Our pets give us so much joy, laughter, and unwavering loyalty throughout their lives; being with them as they pass is my way of giving back a fraction of that boundless love. It's about ensuring they feel safe, cherished, and not alone as they transition peacefully.

My commitment to this choice was powerfully solidified by the loss of my cat, Lucy. We had exhausted every possible measure to keep her with us, but in the end, she was away from home, getting one final "hopeful" treatment, when she died. She died in a hospital surrounded by the loving staff but not with us. That experience left a deep ache in my heart and a profound promise on my lips: I vowed that no other "furry mortal" of ours would ever face that final moment without me by their side. Since then, I've held each of my pets, whispering words of love and gratitude, feeling their last breaths, and ensuring their passing was as peaceful and surrounded by love as possible.

While this is my deeply personal choice, I want to be VERY clear: this is not a path everyone can or should take. The emotional toll of being present during a pet's euthanasia can be immense, and it's a decision each individual must make for themselves. There is absolutely no judgment or shame in not being able to be there. Our pets, with their incredible capacity for love and understanding, know how much we adore them, regardless of how we handle their final goodbye. **The love you share with your pet is vast and transcends that single moment.** They understand your heart, and they know they are loved, whether you are holding them or are in the next room.

In the end, the goal is always the same: to ensure our beloved companions have a peaceful and dignified passing. For me, the quiet strength found in those last moments of shared tenderness is a necessary part of my grieving and healing process. It's how I honor the incredible bond we shared and ensure their last moments are filled with love and warmth.

No Judgment, Only Love

furry mortal

[noun]

A vibrant soul in a temporary coat, whose purpose is to spend every ounce of their finite time teaching us that a life well-lived is measured in wagging tails and shared sunbeams.

Reflection 3

Paw Prints on the Soul

The sudden quiet that follows the departure of a furry mortal is an immense, heavy thing. It is not merely the absence of noise; it is a hollow space carved out exactly where a constant, rhythmic heartbeat used to be. In those first few days and weeks, the silence offers no protection. It provides no defense against the persistent ache of "yesterday." You find yourself performing the rituals of a haunted life—searching the shadows for a familiar shape, or tensing at a tell-tale, hopeful click on the floorboards that your mind insists is real, only to realize it is nothing at all. During this time, memories are not gentle. They are sharp, quick, and jagged, serving as the real, hard lessons that love was always meant to teach us.

To be a fierce advocate for your pet during their life is a noble task, but to be an advocate for your own heart after they are gone is an act of survival. You must let the tears fall. They are never a sign of weakness; they are the final, honest payment on the mortgage of the heart. They are the deepest tribute you can offer to years of pure fidelity. If the bond was great, the grief will be great, and there is a profound, necessary validity in that sorrow. We must allow ourselves the grace to feel the full weight of the silence before we can begin to hear the music that follows it.

Slowly, almost imperceptibly, the edges of that sorrow begin to smooth. The transition from acute pain to persistent grace happens in the stories we finally find the strength to tell. As we move through the holistic journey of grief, we stop pulling only the final, dark, and overwhelming moments forward. We stop obsessing over the "medicalized" ending and begin to remember the "lived" life. We realize that what stays is not the break in the heart, but the rhythm that filled it for so many years.

What lasts is the easy rhythm of a happy walk on a crisp autumn afternoon. It is the residual warmth settled deep in your favorite chair, or the funny, singular way they used to "talk" with those little, excited whimpers that caught the air when they dreamed. These are the paw prints etched into the deepest part of your soul. We often mistake these marks for the tally of a devastating cost, but they are a map. They are the lines that make us whole—a clear, indelible record of a love we lost, which we eventually understand is a love we still possess.

The heart will mend, but it will not be the same heart as it was before. It will be a heart that has grown around a hollow space, incorporating the void into its very structure. It does not forget; it simply matures. It becomes a heart that knows how to whisper a sweet, necessary name with a smile instead of a sob. The legacy of the furry mortal is not that they leave us broken, but that they leave us expanded—capable of carrying both a profound absence and a permanent presence at the same exact time.

Furry Mortals Quality of Life Assessed

Lucy

Zack

Lucy & Zack - Two Very Different Sides of the Same Coin

When I look back at those desperate days with Lucy, the thing that haunts me most is the overwhelming feeling of pure guesswork. We loved fiercely, but we were operating blind, driven only by emotion, desperately trying to divine where the line between care and suffering truly lay. The painful truth is that when we faced those final, critical decisions with all our furry mortals—from Lucy's desperate fight for longevity to the heartbreaking decision to let Zack walk into the clinic for his peaceful farewell—we did not have a formal Quality of Life Assessment Tool in our hands.

We simply didn't have the education to recognize that such an objective, compassionate framework even existed, much less how to use its simple metrics to measure our pets' suffering. If I could go back and give my past self, and all the other loving pet parents who shared their stories in this book, just one thing, it wouldn't be a miraculous cure; it would be the knowledge in these chapters.

It's the clarity that comes from tracking those scores (which I did retroactively to a degree below), realizing that dignity is measurable, and recognizing that we don't have to wait for total collapse to act. This is the education that prevents profound regret, ensuring that your choice, unlike mine with Lucy, is selfless, informed, and the ultimate expression of love, just as it was with Zack's right goodbye.

Side One: Lucy

When I look back at the devastating experience with Lucy, I feel that familiar, sharp wave of regret. We were so blinded by the possibility of buying her more time—forcing her tiny body through transfusions and feedings to keep her weight up—that we simply missed what a QOL Assessment Tool would have been screaming at us if we had known about them.

I realize now that her Physical Well-being scores were likely in the danger zone for months. Her Appetite would have scored a crippling '1' due to the force-feeding, and despite all our efforts, her underlying heart and cancer struggles meant her Pain & Comfort scores were chronically low.

We kept fighting the disease, but in doing so, we unwittingly demolished her emotional well-being scores. The stress of constant clinic visits and aggressive treatments meant her happiness and joy score would have steadily plummeted, showing us that her spirit was withdrawing long before her body gave out. The true tragedy, the final sting of regret, is we completely felt we failed her because she died alone during a transfusion, turning our intense love into a source of lasting, unnecessary trauma. **This is exactly the kind of heartbreaking, blurred line between love and suffering that I created a QOL tool to prevent.**

Side Two: Zack

And on the other side of this coin is Zack, our magnificent Border Collie, and the QOL tool doesn't bring regret; it brings me a profound sense of peace. When I apply it to how we handled things in the end for him, it shows me that we honored our commitment to his dignity right up to his final breath. And although we still were unaware of these tools, we used our own framework as a loving compass, not an emergency siren.

While his physical well-being score would have clearly indicated the effects of his long life as his mobility was slipping, and his once-graceful walk was labored, we noticed that his pain and comfort scores were still manageable, reflecting a life lived mostly free of chronic suffering.

Most importantly, Zack's emotional well-being remained beautifully high. He was still "Zack," still spirited, still engaged, meaning his happiness and social interaction scores were not yet compromised. This is what helped us identify the moment before his spirit would have broken or his bad days would have begun to consistently outnumber the good.

By making the choice while he could still walk into the clinic that day and surrounded by love, we ensured his final score was exemplary. **This allowed us to provide the right goodbye. A peaceful, dignified transition that remains the ultimate, selfless act of love.**

Step-By-Step User Guide

The creation of this assessment tool was a way for me to take this book's philosophy and turn it into a practical, actionable guide. While the book highlights the need for a compassionate end-of-life approach, a simple story is not enough to help a grieving pet parent navigate this incredibly difficult decision. This tool was designed to be that bridge. It's an objective framework to move beyond emotional turmoil and turn your intuitive feelings into documented observations. By giving you a way to evaluate your pet's physical, emotional, and social well-being in a structured way, this assessment helps you confidently make a decision so you can be at peace with knowing you've honored the precious bond you share.

How to Use the Furry Mortals Quality of Life Assessment

Think of the Furry Mortals Quality of Life Assessment as an ongoing conversation, not a one-time test. Its main goal is to give you a clear, structured way to document your pet's daily condition. This tool helps you start important discussions with your family and your vet, bridging the gap between your intimate knowledge of your pet and your vet's clinical expertise. It's not a replacement for professional advice or a diagnostic tool; it's a guided reflection to help you feel more confident and involved in your pet's care.

Understanding the Scoring System

The assessment uses a simple 1-10 scoring system for each category, where a higher score means your pet has a better quality of life. This system is meant to be easy to use even when you're going through a tough emotional time.

When you score each item, be honest about your observations from the past few days.

- **A score of 1** means your pet is experiencing a severe or unmanageable issue in that area.
- **A score of 5** is a neutral or questionable point, which means you need to pay closer attention to this area or consider taking action.
- **A score of 10** means your pet is doing excellent, with no signs of struggle.

Each category also has a "Notes" column. Remember, your personal observations are often more revealing than a simple number, so use this space to add details about what you're seeing.

Section A: Physical Comfort (The Body)

This part of the assessment is all about your pet's Physical Comfort. Combining the best metrics from top vet scales (see *Works Used To Create Assessment Tool*) helps you get specific about your worries, so you can turn them into actionable observations for your vet.

- **Pain & Comfort:** This is a huge one. Your pet can't feel peace or dignity if they're in constant pain. Sometimes the signs are subtle, like trembling or just being restless when they should be relaxing. You might also notice they're avoiding certain touches or their posture has changed. This is where we check if their pain is under control with their current treatment plan.
- **Mobility & Movement:** How well can your pet get around? Do they need help walking or standing up? Are they suddenly hesitant to go on walks or tackle the stairs? A pet that used to be active but is now struggling with simple movement is likely experiencing a big drop in their quality of life.
- **Appetite & Hydration:** Pay close attention to your pet's interest in food and water. If they're no longer excited about meals or treats, or if they've become picky, it's a red flag.

Also, note if they're drinking way more or less than usual, as that could point to an underlying health issue.

- **Respiration:** Breathing difficulties are a sure sign of a suffering pet. Look at their breathing patterns. Are they panting while resting? Are you hearing any coughing or wheezing? A pet that's having a hard time breathing is suffering, plain and simple.

- **Hygiene & Cleanliness:** This is about your pet's ability to stay clean and manage their own body. If they're unable to control their bladder or bowels or are too weak to move away from their own waste, it's a clear loss of dignity and comfort. An unkempt, matted coat can also be a sign that they're too sick to groom themselves.

Section B: Happiness and Inner World (The Spirit)

This part of the assessment is all about your pet's Happiness and Inner World (their spirit). Their emotional well-being is just as important as their physical health, especially toward the end of their life. This section helps you look at the non-physical signs that show how your pet is truly feeling.

- **Happiness & Joy:** Does your pet still find enjoyment in their day-to-day life? Think about the things they used to love. Do they still get a little spark of interest from their favorite toy, or do they still seek out a sunny spot on the floor for a nap? Even small moments of happiness matter. If your pet seems dull, depressed, or just apathetic about things they once loved, it could be a sign of significant emotional or psychological suffering that is lowering their quality of life.

- **Social Interaction:** The bond you share with your pet is incredibly important. In this section, we look at whether your pet is still connecting with you and the rest of the family. A pet that used to love cuddling but now withdraws, hides, or seems irritable when you approach might be in pain or scared. On the other hand, it's also worth noting if a pet who was very independent their whole life now seeks more closeness or attention. These changes in social behavior can tell you a lot about their inner experience.

- **Demeanor & Cognition:** As pets get older, their minds can change, too. You might notice signs of cognitive decline, like confusion or disorientation, especially in the evening or at night. A pet might begin to wander aimlessly or get stuck in a corner. If your pet's personality seems to have changed or they appear disconnected from their surroundings, they might be experiencing a form of suffering that isn't addressed by physical pain management alone. Noticing these shifts can help you provide a more comfortable and supportive environment for them.

Section C: Environmental & Caregiver Well-being (The Sanctuary)

This part of the assessment recognizes a simple, but profound truth: your pet's Quality of Life isn't an isolated metric. It's deeply intertwined with its home environment (their sanctuary) and your family's ability to care for it. This holistic perspective is what makes our tool a true companion to the book, as it addresses the **needs of you and your pet together** during these final, precious days.

- **Home Comfort:** Your home should be your pet's sanctuary, a place where they feel safe and secure. Here, we ask you to think about whether you've made changes to meet your pet's changing needs. Have you installed ramps or stairs to help them with mobility? Are their food and water bowls raised to a more comfortable height so they don't have to strain? Have you put down non-slip mats or rugs to prevent falls? These simple modifications can make a world of difference, reducing their pain, anxiety, and distress. Creating a comforting space for your pet is a beautiful act of love.
- **Caregiver Capacity (The "YOU" Factor):** Your well-being is a direct and critical factor in your pet's quality of life. The

JOURNEYS scale wisely points out that if a caregiver is constantly worried, overwhelmed, or financially strained, it can take a toll on the quality of care they're able to provide. This part of the assessment gently prompts you to be honest with yourself about your emotional, physical, and financial capacity. This isn't about judgment; it's about acknowledging your own needs so that you can continue to provide consistent, loving attention. As the author's friend Jill's story with Mia teaches us, even with the best intentions, the end-of-life journey can leave lasting emotional wounds if we don't acknowledge and prepare for our own needs.

- **Proactive Planning (The "UNCERTAINTY" Factor):** The absence of a proactive plan can lead to panicked, reactive decisions during a crisis. And in those moments, it's easy for both you and your pet to suffer. This is why we encourage you to have open and honest discussions with your veterinarian about "what if" scenarios, such as a sudden decline or unmanageable pain. By having a clear understanding of your pet's condition and the available options, you can face the end-of-life with greater confidence and less anxiety. This planning isn't about giving up; it's about giving yourselves a clear path forward, ensuring you can honor your pet's life with peace and dignity, even when the road ahead is uncertain.

Understanding the Scores

For this assessment tool to truly help you, it's best to use it as a consistent, loving practice, not just a one-time event. Following these steps can help you get the most out of it and feel confident in your observations:

- **Start Early and Track Regularly:** This assessment is most powerful when you use it to gently track trends over time. Try to start as soon as your pet is diagnosed with a chronic illness or when you first notice them slowing down with age. Filling it out daily or weekly, depending on how your pet is doing, will help you build a visual record of their journey. This can make it easier to see subtle changes and help you feel more prepared.

- **Capture a Full Picture:** Your pet's quality of life can change throughout the day, so it's a great idea to complete the assessment at different times. For example, your pet might be more mobile and playful in the morning but seem more tired and uncomfortable in the evening. Capturing these different moments gives you a more complete picture of their well-being.

- **Collaborate with Your Family:** If you have a few people helping with your pet's care, it can be really helpful for each person to fill out the assessment on their own. Comparing notes and scores can lead to a productive, heartfelt conversation and help everyone feel aligned on how your pet is really doing.

- **Rely on the Notes Column:** The number score is a helpful snapshot, but your personal notes are often the most revealing part. Use the Notes column to write down specific changes in your pet's behavior, mood, or physical symptoms. For instance, instead of just giving a score of 7 for mobility, you might write, *"Hesitates before getting on the couch, but can still jump with a little encouragement."* These details can be so helpful when you talk with your vet.

Interpreting Your Scores: Finding the Tipping Point

Interpreting your pet's scores is a deeply personal and nuanced process. There are no hard and fast rules for making a final decision, but the data you collect is your anchor against emotional bias. **The goal of this assessment isn't to give you a definitive yes or no answer.** Instead, it's designed to help you gently identify the "tipping point"—that moment when the bad days consistently start to outnumber the good ones.

A single low score in a critical area, like constant pain or difficulty breathing, can be a more significant sign of suffering than a moderate decline across many different areas. If you see a total score that drops below a certain threshold or if a score in a critical area stays consistently low, that's your signal to have a serious, compassionate conversation with your veterinarian.

This assessment helps you understand your pet's decline and find the courage to prepare for the final decisions.

The Power of the Good Day vs. Bad Day Calendar

A wonderful complement to the assessment tool is a simple **Good vs. Bad Day Calendar.** While the numerical scores give you a structured look at your pet's well-being, a calendar offers a beautiful, visual representation of their journey. The idea is simple: each day, you just mark it with a "Good Day" or "Bad Day" symbol.

A "good day" is one where your pet seems comfortable and happy, enjoys their favorite activities, and has a positive demeanor. A "bad day" is one where they are in pain, withdrawn, or struggling with basic functions. This method helps you move beyond the emotions of the moment. On a particularly good day, it's easy to forget the tough days that came before. But this visual calendar provides a clear, tangible record that can gently show you when the bad days are starting to outnumber the good ones. When you combine this visual record with the detailed notes from your assessment, it paints an undeniable picture of your pet's journey. This can help your family come together and find a sense of peace and consensus about the right time to say goodbye. It's a way to lovingly honor their story until the very end.

Preparing for the Veterinary Conversation

This assessment isn't just a document; it's a tool designed to prepare you for what we hope will be an essential partnership with your veterinary team. When it's time to meet with your veterinarian, bringing the completed assessment and the good vs. bad day calendar isn't just about sharing data—it's about opening a compassionate, collaborative conversation.

You can walk into the clinic and say, *"We've been using this tool to lovingly track our pet's well-being, and here are the trends we've been seeing."* This simple act transforms the dynamic from a passive one into an active partnership. It ensures that any final decisions you make are based on a shared, comprehensive understanding of your pet's condition.

This book calls for open communication, and this tool helps you do exactly that. It gives you a way to ask those difficult, but necessary, questions with more confidence, like, *"What are the ethical considerations of continuing treatment?"* or *"Can you walk us through the euthanasia process step-by-step so we know what to expect and can prepare for it?"*

This proactive, honest dialogue, rooted in a shared commitment to your pet's dignity and peace, transforms a heartbreaking conversation into a collaborative act of compassion. **It's about facing this difficult moment together, for your pet.**

Printing the Worksheet

This worksheet is designed to be a printable resource for you to evaluate your pet's quality of life. You can download a printable copy here:

HTTPS://WWW.FURRYMORTALS.COM/QOL

Complete the following assessment daily or weekly, scoring each criterion on a scale of 1-10.

- 1: Poor/Severe Deficiency (The worst it can be)
- 5: Questionable/Neutral (Uncertainty or some decline)
- 10: Excellent/No Concerns (The best it can be)

Use the notes section to provide specific, qualitative observations. This worksheet should be used to track trends over time and guide conversations with your veterinarian and family.

Section A:
Physical Well-being

_/_/_

PAIN & COMFORT

Is pain well-managed? Is the pet trembling, panting, or restless at rest?

MOBILITY & MOVEMENT

Can the pet stand and walk unassisted? Does it have difficulty navigating stairs or its environment?

APPETITE & HYDRATION

Is the pet eating and drinking normally? Is it still interested in treats?

RESPIRATION

Is breathing difficult, labored or excessively fast, especially at rest?

HYGIENE & CLEANLINESS

Can the pet keep itself clean? Does it have accidents? Is its coat unkempt?

Section B:
Emotional Well-being

__/__/__

HAPPINESS & JOY

Does the pet still enjoy life? Is there interest in toys, play, or other favorite activities?

SOCIAL INTERACTION

Is the pet still engaging with family? Or is it withdrawn, irritable, or seeking solitude?

DEMEANOR & COGNITION

Does the pet seem confused, disoriented, or apathetic? Is there restlessness or aimless wandering?

FURRY MORTALS QUALITY OF LIFE ASSESSMENT TOOL

Section C:
Environmental & Caregiver Well-being

HOME COMFORT

Has the home environment been adapted for comfort and safety (e.g., ramps, non-slip mats, raised bowls)?

CAREGIVER CAPACITY

Is the caregiver feeling overwhelmed, stressed, or financially strained by the demands of care?

PROACTIVE PLANNING

Has the family discussed "what if" scenarios and end-of-life options with the veterinarian?

___/___/___

TODAY'S SCORE

Put the average of the numbers in your score column to represent your pet's current overall quality of life today.

The Oliver Project   240

Questions of the Heart

Oliver & Zack

Not All the Answers, But Some

The following section addresses the most immediate and profound questions we face during the end-of-life journey, anchoring compassionate guidance in objectivity and empathetic validation.

I. The Agonizing Question: Determining the Right Time

Q: **How will we know when it's the right time to use euthanasia for our pet?**

That ultimate question "How will we know when it's the right time to give our pet a peaceful passing?"—is, perhaps, the most agonizing query born from profound love. The weight of this decision is immense, and the answer rarely comes as a single, clear-cut moment. Instead, it is a conclusion we reach through objective assessment and compassionate observation over time.

The core principle is shifting our focus from simply prolonging life to maximizing comfort and dignity. Our goal is not to find the perfect second, but to prevent the worst pain and distress. For our beloved companion, the kindest choice is often made slightly too soon rather than moments too late, ensuring their final departure is peaceful. When faced with this decision, euthanasia must be reframed not as a failure, but as the final, most selfless act of love—the ultimate way to prevent prolonged suffering when their quality of life is irreversibly compromised. The objective assessment tools are critical because they act as a necessary emotional counterweight, liberating us from the emotional paralysis that often delays the decision.

To help us move past the subjective nature of emotion and gain clarity, the use of objective anchors is imperative. This framework, based on the Six Pillars of Quality of Life, transforms intuitive feelings into documented observations. This objective data is the strongest anchor against the tidal wave of grief and fear.

- **Pain & Comfort:** The primary indicator of declining quality of life. Suffering cannot be managed if pain breaks through medication, causing restlessness, reluctance to move, or aggressive guarding.

- **Appetite & Hydration:** A significant measure of dignity. The pet should be willingly taking in nourishment. When eating becomes a struggle or they refuse favorite treats consistently, their quality of life is severely compromised.

- **Happiness & Joy:** This pillar measures the pet's spirit. Are they still engaging with their world? Do they still purr, seek a sunbeam, or acknowledge their family? A dull or apathetic demeanor signals a spirit that is withdrawn, indicating psychological suffering.

- **Mobility & Hygiene:** A pet must be able to move and maintain cleanliness without painful struggle. The inability to stand unassisted, repeated falls, or loss of bowel/bladder control requiring constant cleaning are clear markers of lost dignity.

- **Respiration:** Breathing difficulties are a non-negotiable sign of suffering. If the pet is panting while resting or struggling for air, distress is profound and immediate.

- **Social Interaction:** This measures the strength of the bond. Are they still connecting with the family, or are they hiding, withdrawn, or irritable? Changes in social behavior are direct expressions of their inner experience.

The most powerful objective tool at our disposal is the Good Days vs. Bad Days Log. This involves using a simple calendar to mark each day as either "Good" (comfortable, ate well) or "Bad" (in pain, withdrawn, significant distress). The definitive "tipping point" is reached when the bad days consistently begin to outweigh the good days over a period of

7 to 10 days. This visual record provides the courage we need to act with compassion. Proactive discussion is essential: we must talk to our veterinarian or Comfort Care caregiver before a crisis, defining clear, non-negotiable markers for the end, transforming the difficult decision from emotional chaos into a path of foresight.

Q: How will we know the difference between our pet sleeping peacefully and them having passed away?

As loving pet parents, the heavy anxiety of mistaking a deep, peaceful sleep for the final surrender is common. This profound moment, when the spirit moves on, leaves the physical body still. We must rely on objective signs to confirm the transition is complete. This knowledge serves as vital emotional preparation for us.

The following three signs distinguish death from even the deepest rest, eliminating the trauma of uncertainty:

- **Absence of Heartbeat and Respiration:** This is the most primary confirmation. Place a hand firmly over the pet's ribcage, just behind the front elbow, and look and feel intently for any rise and fall of the chest or the faint pulse of the heart. If absolutely no breath or heart movement is observed for a full minute, the transition has occurred.

- **Fixed and Unresponsive Eyes:** Unlike a pet in deep sleep, a pet who has passed will have eyes that remain open, fixed, and unblinking. The pupils will often be widely dilated, and the eyes may appear slightly dry or glazed over. A gentle touch to the corner of the eye will elicit no reflex or blink, confirming the cessation of brain function.

- **Complete Loss of Muscle Tension:** After death, every muscle immediately relaxes, leading to an instantaneous, profound stillness. The body will feel heavy and entirely limp, without any ability to brace or hold a position. This final, utter relaxation may also lead to the release of urine or stool—a completely normal, non-aware natural body reflex.

Providing explicit details about post-mortem physical realities—such as the eyes remaining open, possible agonal gasping, or the voiding of fluids—is a necessary component of helping you find peace. Knowing these are reflexes and not signs of pain ensures that the emotional memory of the passing is one of quiet confirmation, rather than fear. Once these signs are observed, we must give ourselves permission to pause, accepting that the greatest love of our furry mortal's life—our presence—is the final comfort they received.

II. Navigating the Emotional Terrain: Validation and Support

Q: Is it normal for us to feel so much grief over our pet?

Losing a furry mortal, our confidante, and a source of unconditional love, is one of the most profound heartbreaks a human will ever experience. When the silence descends, the pain can be so overwhelming that we might ask if our grief is "too much" or "normal." The answer is a resounding **yes**—our feelings are absolutely valid.

The unique ache we feel comes from the loss of a legitimate, deeply held relationship; a pet is never "just an animal"; they were family, structure, and unconditional love distilled. The sorrow is compounded by the experience of disenfranchised grief, the silent layer of pain that arises when society minimizes the loss with phrases like, "It was just a pet," which forces us to feel isolated and doubt the validity of our own pain. The void stems from losing not only their physical presence but the sudden, jarring absence of our entire shared life—the daily rituals, the silent emotional support, and the purpose derived from caregiving.

The intensity of grief is intrinsically linked to the sudden Post-Caregiver Void. The intense, purposeful energy we dedicated to caregiving (medications, special diets, routines) is instantly stripped away, leaving us with a sense of aimlessness that exacerbates sorrow and can lead to an identity crisis. The ache is intensified by the "Weight of the Should Have"—the self-inflicted guilt that accompanies loss, born from holding ourselves to impossible standards of perfect caregiving.

There is no set timeline for healing, and the process is unique. We must be encouraged to practice self-compassion and allow ourselves to feel our pain without judgment. To actively counter the pain of 20/20 hindsight, a powerful technique is to create a tangible inventory of love—a simple list detailing all the ways care was shown: the vet visits, the specialty food, the cuddles, and the midnight treats. This evidence of care helps balance the overwhelming subjective guilt. To manage the Post-Caregiver Void, we can be advised to redirect the intense, focused energy of caregiving into new, intentional activities, such as volunteering at a local shelter in the pet's memory or resuming a neglected hobby. This transformation of sorrow into a powerful, living tribute ensures the love remains a source of strength, rather than a painful memory of lost purpose.

Q: How Do We Help Our Child Cope With Losing a Pet?

The loss of a furry mortal is often a child's first, raw encounter with death, and their small hearts grapple with tough questions. The most powerful action a parent can take is to be the emotional anchor, helping the child navigate this challenging, essential rite of passage.

Parents must commit to validating, not minimizing, the child's grief. We should allow the child to express all feelings—sadness, confusion, anger, or even indifference—and assure them that these emotions are valid and normal. If the child is not ready to speak, we should not pressure them, respecting their individual timeline for processing sorrow.

To help the child find essential closure, a memorial or burial service can be deeply meaningful. We should discuss the idea with the child and, if they are open to it, allow them to participate fully: sharing a favorite memory, saying final words, or choosing a special item to be included with the remains. This active participation provides a sense of honoring their companion. A parent can facilitate healthy, non-verbal healing through creative expression. Encouraging the child to draw a picture, build a memory box for the pet's collar or tag, or compose a letter to their pet provides a cathartic release for complex feelings that are difficult to articulate with words.

It must be recognized that grief does not follow a schedule. If a child's sadness persists and actively interrupts their daily function, sleep, school performance, or general happiness for an extended period, it is important to seek additional support from a school counselor or a therapist who specializes in children's grief. The loss is a profound teaching moment about love and loss, and a parent's consistent presence and support ensure the child processes their grief in a healthy way.

Q: What support resources (hotlines, groups, counseling) are available to help us cope with intense grief immediately after the loss?

The unique, acute grief that follows the loss of a cherished companion can be a devastating and isolating experience. We must be assured that we are absolutely not alone; a compassionate, understanding community of support exists, dedicated to validating our pain.

In the immediate aftermath, when the shock is deepest, the most accessible lifeline is the ASPCA National Pet Loss Hotline: 877-474-3310. This free nationwide service is staffed by trained professionals or experienced volunteers who offer immediate emotional first aid. The hotline provides a safe, non-judgmental space where we can share our pain, guilt, and disbelief, ensuring a steady, compassionate voice is available to anchor us during those dark, lonely hours.

For sustained, healing support that acknowledges the complexity of mourning, we should seek out support groups. Pet loss support groups, available both locally and virtually (such as the Furry Mortals Online Support Group), create a dedicated space for sharing specific heartache and feeling understood by others who have walked the same path. This communal grieving validates our experience and transforms isolation into shared understanding. Organizations like the International Association for Animal Hospice and Palliative Care (IAAHPC) offer invaluable resources and referrals to certified professionals dedicated to Comfort Care.

If the grief feels paralyzing, prolonged, or is accompanied by intense guilt or symptoms of depression, professional help is a necessary act of self-care. It is advisable to seek a grief counselor or therapist who specializes in pet loss. These professionals understand the disenfranchised nature of this grief and can provide expert tools to help integrate the loss in a healthy way. The veterinary clinic and the crematorium serve as reliable guides and essential hubs for resources, typically providing curated lists of hotlines, local support groups, and counseling referrals.

III. The Act of Compassion: Euthanasia and Immediate Logistics

Q: **The Gentle Transition Explained: What is the step-by-step process, and will our pet feel pain?**

Euthanasia, which literally means "good death," is designed by veterinarians to be a peaceful, gentle, and entirely painless procedure for a beloved companion. The goal is to allow our pet to transition without anxiety, distress, or discomfort. We must be secure in the knowledge that we are providing the ultimate relief from suffering.

The process typically involves two main stages, ensuring comfort and a peaceful passing:

- **Sedation and Relaxation:** In most cases, a sedative or tranquilizer is administered first, usually via an intramuscular injection that feels similar to a routine vaccination. This allows the pet to relax, letting go of any fear, anxiety, or pain, drifting gently into a deep sleep within minutes. This initial quiet time is often the most important part for the pet parent, allowing us to say our final goodbyes in a serene state.
- **The Final Injection:** Once the pet is completely sedated and sleeping soundly, the veterinarian administers the final solution—a high concentration of a gentle sleeping

medication (often a barbiturate). Administered intravenously, the large dose quickly causes **immediate, deep unconsciousness**, gently stopping the heart and breathing. The process is extremely rapid, usually taking only 10 to 30 seconds after the injection is complete.

Managing Physical Reactions and Trauma Mitigation

It is important to understand the normal, involuntary post-mortem movements that may occur after the injection, as they are often misinterpreted as signs of pain. These are mere reflexes and do not indicate the pet is aware or suffering: minor muscle twitches, one or two final, deep "agonal" gasps, and the eyes remaining open. Knowing this beforehand minimizes the likelihood of us experiencing an emotional trigger during the aftermath.

A specific warning must be integrated. The profound muscle relaxation following the sedative can cause the pet to become instantly and completely limp. We choosing in-home euthanasia must consciously prepare for this physical reality by positioning ourselves and our pet securely (e.g., on a low bed or floor, braced against a firm object) before the sedative is administered. This proactive measure prevents the traumatic shock of the pet inadvertently falling, ensuring the memory of the passing is peaceful and dignified.

Q: What options are available for handling our pet's body immediately after they pass at home, and who should we call first?

When the final breath is taken, our focus must remain on the emotional transfer—the loving goodbye. Once that moment has passed, the sacred task of the physical transfer must be addressed.

The very first action, once we are ready, is to call our established veterinary office or a dedicated pet funeral home or crematorium. These professionals are specialists in this tender transition and are equipped to handle the call with immediate, nonjudgemental compassion. It is important to communicate pre-planned wishes immediately ("My beloved pet has passed away at home, and we have arranged for private cremation"). This clarity allows them to bypass unnecessary discussion and focus directly on coordinating the next steps.

While waiting for transport, the immediate preparation becomes our final, intimate act of care, ensuring the pet travels with dignity.

- **Collect Keepsakes:** First, collect any keepsakes desired—a final fur clipping, a paw print, or their collar. Once the body is moved, these opportunities vanish.
- **Gentle Positioning:** The pet must be gently positioned onto a thick blanket or towel. This must be completed quickly (within the first one to two hours) because rigor mortis sets in rapidly, which can complicate respectful handling and prevent the body from being positioned in a peaceful, natural posture.
- **Wrapping:** Carefully and completely wrap the pet's body in their favorite soft blanket or a clean sheet.

Whether the pet is picked up by a professional transport vehicle or carefully placed in our own car for the final drive, these steps ensure the transition is handled with the utmost reverence.

Q: **How Long Can We Reasonably Wait Before Making Final Arrangements?**

After a companion passes, the world stands still, and the desire not to rush the goodbye is profound. Fortunately, we do have a little time before rushing into final arrangements. In a home environment, the most respectful timeframe for making and executing the final transfer plans is within about 4 to 6 hours. This allows for a period of private grieving while ensuring the next steps are taken with dignity.

If more time is needed, we can extend this window by utilizing cooling methods. This involves gently positioning the body, wrapping it in a blanket, and placing ice packs over the abdomen and chest. This simple step can buy several extra hours to call the veterinarian or pet crematorium and finalize the logistics of the transfer, but it is strongly advised not to delay past the next morning. The necessity of managing the transfer for hygienic and respectful reasons dictates the timeframe. Having a clear Crisis Protocol established beforehand ensures that indecision doesn't turn this tender moment into a crisis.

IV. Financial Clarity: Transparency and Planning

Q: **How will we pay for the end-of-life services, and what is the range of total cost we should be prepared for?**

The final chapter with a cherished companion requires addressing the subject of **cost**. The unique emotional distress of pet loss must never be compounded by financial panic; clarity and foresight in financial planning are a necessary act of maturity and love.

We must anticipate that end-of-life expenses will generally be categorized into two distinct, non-overlapping services:

- **The Veterinary Fee:** This covers the professional act of euthanasia and any necessary medication (like sedation). This fee is paid directly to the veterinary clinic or the home-hospice service. An in-home euthanasia service, which provides unparalleled peace and comfort, will naturally carry a **higher fee**, factoring in travel time and specialized staffing, compared to a procedure performed at the clinic.

- **The Aftercare Fee:** This cost covers the disposition of the pet's body and is paid to the crematorium or pet funeral home. This fee is determined primarily by the choice of memorialization and the pet's size/weight. **Communal cremation** is the most affordable option, as the remains are mixed and not returned. **Individual or private cremation** is substantially more expensive, as it guarantees the return of only the pet's ashes, requiring a meticulous, dedicated process.

The total expenditure—combining the Veterinary Fee and the Aftercare Fee—can range widely, from a few hundred dollars for a small pet receiving basic services, to upwards of a thousand dollars for a large pet receiving specialized in-home care and private cremation.

To manage this range of expenses without emotional crisis, we must first:

- **Ask for an Itemized Quote:** We must not accept vague estimates. It is necessary to contact the chosen vet and crematorium separately and ask for a detailed, itemized breakdown of the total cost based on the pet's weight and the specific services selected (e.g., in-home service with private cremation).
- **Plan for Payment Flexibility:** Knowing the payment logistics beforehand is essential. While most services accept credit cards, those facing a crisis without immediate funds should inquire about short-term payment plans or third-party financing options specializing in veterinary care.

Proactive financial planning, such as establishing a Dedicated Dignity Fund, is the ultimate act of preventative love. This ensures that the final decision is guided solely by compassion and the pet's quality of life, rather than being forced prematurely by financial hardship.

V. Honoring Legacy: Aftercare and Memorialization

Q: Can We Be Buried with Our Pet?

The desire to be buried alongside a beloved companion is the ultimate way to honor the unconditional love and promise to be together until the very end. This profound wish recognizes pets as the kin they truly are.

While most traditional cemeteries remain restrictive, the landscape is slowly changing. The legal truth—that a pet is property under the law, and a Will alone is insufficient—demands the elevated legal structure of a Pet Trust.

The best solution is often cremation, which offers the most flexibility, allowing the remains of both human and animal to be commingled or placed with theirs in a single urn for a joint placement. We are advised to secure this arrangement by researching local laws and cemetery policies and, most importantly, discussing and setting these wishes into our final legal documents now.

Q: How do we choose between private, individual or communal pet cremation?

Grief arrives with a thousand decisions, and choosing our pet's final arrangements is one of the most tender and challenging. The choice between having our pet's physical remains returned to us (Private or Individual) or not (Communal) rests entirely on our personal needs for closure and memorialization.

- **Private Cremation:** Your pet is the only animal in the cremation chamber throughout the entire process. This offers the highest level of exclusivity and sacred space. It is the most expensive option, chosen by those who want total certainty that their pet's final journey is completely solitary.

- **Individual Cremation:** Multiple pets are in the chamber at once, but they are kept strictly separated by physical dividers. This prevents any commingling, ensuring you receive only your pet's remains. This is a respectful middle ground for those who want a tangible memorial but at a more accessible price point than a private service.

- **Communal Cremation:** Pets are cremated together in a collective group without separation. Because remains are commingled, ashes are not returned to the family; instead, they are usually scattered by the facility in a memorial garden. This is the most affordable path, chosen by those who find closure through memories rather than physical remains.

The critical decision point is the need for a physical anchor. If we require a physical item to focus our grief, individual cremation is the clearer path. However, a practical, cost-mitigating strategy exists: if communal cremation is chosen, we should still request a paw print, a fur clipping, or a nose print from the veterinarian or the cremation service before the process begins. These cherished keepsakes offer a tangible, enduring touchpoint without the higher cost of the ashes themselves.

Q: Are there local or state regulations we need to be aware of if we plan to bury our pet at home?

The impulse to bury a cherished companion in our own garden is a natural, heartfelt desire to transform a piece of land into sacred ground. However, before we commit to this final, permanent choice, we must understand that local and state laws frequently govern home burial to protect public health and water quality.

It is mandatory to pause and consult local town or county ordinances and state environmental regulations. These regulations typically require a minimum depth of burial to prevent scavenging and dictate critical location restrictions. The grave must be a specific, significant distance from any natural water sources (streams, wells) to prevent contamination, and also a minimum distance from property lines. We must consider the immense emotional weight of home burial: if the family ever moves, we will be leaving the pet's final resting spot behind, which can intensify grief.

Q: What Are Some Tangible Ways to Memorialize Our Furry Mortal?

Memorialization is the courageous, final act of love that transforms paralyzing grief into enduring tribute, ensuring the pet's footprint on the heart is permanent. We crave something real, something tangible, to hold onto.

Intimate Keepsakes: Pieces of the Physical

Before the companion leaves care, essential, simple items can be collected that hold monumental emotional weight:

- **Paw Prints and Nose Prints:** These are direct, irrefutable records of their unique identity. A paw print allows us to feel the texture of their pad again, and a nose print is unique, like a human fingerprint. Memorial services can convert these prints into personalized jewelry or plaques.

- **Fur Clippings:** A small lock of their fur is one of the most intimate physical reminders, often retaining their familiar scent. This can be tucked into a locket or a keepsake bag, providing a piece of them to hold.

- **Collar or Tag:** The collar they wore for years is a relic of their daily life. This can be framed alongside a picture or simply hung, allowing the familiar tag to jingle slightly.

Memorials Infused with Ashes

If individual cremation is chosen, modern options allow for the artistic integration of their remains, fulfilling the need for a sustained connection:

- **Cremation Jewelry:** Artisans can integrate a tiny portion of the ashes into glass, resin, or precious metal, transforming the remains into stunning, wearable tributes that serve as an enduring source of comfort.

- **Biodegradable Urns:** These allow the ashes to be buried with a tree seed, nourishing a new, living memorial. The tree becomes a physical continuation of the life cherished.

Ongoing and Living Tributes

A memorial does not have to be a static object; it can be a living, purposeful tribute:

- **The Memory Box:** Designate a special container for all their treasures (toys, leash, tags). Creating this box is a healing ritual that allows us to consciously gather and curate our shared history.

- **Donations in Their Name:** Transforming grief into compassionate action by donating to a local shelter or rescue organization ensures the pet's legacy continues to support other animals in need.

- **The Subtle Anchor:** The practice of keeping our furry mortals' tags on our keychain demonstrates how subtle gestures ensure the beloved companion's spirit remains an active, cherished part of daily life.

Q: How can we manage the physical reminders of our pet's absence?

Losing a pet leaves behind a home steeped in them—the empty bed, the half-eaten treats, and that specific spot on the couch that always held their shape. These are more than just objects; they are emotional landmarks that carry intense sensory memory (scent, the ghost sound of a collar) and can trigger overwhelming waves of grief every time they are encountered.

There is no "right" way to handle clearing out these things—only the way that feels right for us. The first step is to implement The Ritual of the Box: carefully packing each item—the worn collar, the threadbare blanket, the loved toy—into a "box of essence" to contain the physical remnants of the life adored.

We must then decide how to process these artifacts:

- **Cherished Keepsakes:** Some items, like the collar or a special toy, can be reserved as keepsakes for a memory box or a respectful shelf, offering comfort, not pain.
- **Transforming Pain into Compassion:** If there are quality items that we cannot bear to discard, donation to a local animal shelter is a beautiful act that transforms pain into compassion, bringing comfort to an animal in need.
- **The Pause:** If the decision is too much, we can gather the items, neatly box them up, and store them out of sight until the rawness of the loss softens.

Healing is not about erasing the pet's presence, but about transforming that presence from a source of sharp pain into one of deep, abiding love.

Oliver

The Oliver Project   260

Epilogue

Navigating the end of a pet's life has been, for me, an intensely personal and emotional journey. It is a path forged in the raw, aching reality of experiences like the frantic, misguided fight for Lucy's longevity, and the profound, peaceful foresight found in preparing for Zack's dignified farewell.

Through the stories and the lessons shared in this book, and inspired by the profound principles of *Being Mortal*, I've come to understand that we can shift our focus from solely prolonging life to instead prioritizing comfort, well-being, and the precious bond we share with our animal companions.

A Call for Peace, Not Perfection

The core of our journey is the Compassion Contract—a selfless promise to honor our pet's dignity above our own future grief. It requires a conscious shift in perspective: recognizing that for our furry mortals, there is only the quality of life *now*.

We have seen how objective tools, like the Furry Mortals QOL Assessment, and the simple yet undeniable clarity of the Good Days vs. Bad Days Log, can transform emotional paralysis into confident, compassionate action. The goal is not to find the perfect second, but to prevent the worst pain and distress. The kindest choice is often made slightly too soon rather than moments too late, ensuring their final departure is peaceful.

The Legacy We Leave Behind

This guide has been my attempt to explore the various facets of holistic end-of-life care: from creating a comfortable home sanctuary and utilizing gentle therapies, to making compassionate decisions about euthanasia, and finding ways to support ourselves through the inevitable grieving process.

I've learned that by recognizing the interconnectedness of a pet's physical, emotional, and environmental needs, we can truly strive to provide a peaceful and meaningful end-of-life experience that honors the unique life and love of each cherished member of our family.

The paw prints etched into the deepest part of your soul are not the tally marks of a devastating cost. They are the map. The lines that make you whole. What endures is the assurance that when their spirit started to roam, they were wrapped in the unconditional love and peace they deserved, leaving you with the quiet, overwhelming gratitude of knowing you honored their final moments.

May you look back on your shared experience with a sense of peace and pride, knowing you honored your pet with the best possible care until the very end.

Dedicated to the indelible bond and the promise of a peaceful farewell.

Afterword

The journey through writing this book—a deep dive into the pain and peace of final goodbyes—has been profoundly shaped by the spirits of those who have gone before. But the ultimate testament to the legacy they left is found in the joy of those who remain and those who arrive after the grief begins to soften.

I dedicate this final reflection to our current companions, **Murphy & Zander**, and our latest furry mortal, **Ozwald**. He is a testament to the enduring human capacity to love again, even after the heart has been broken and painstakingly mended.

Ozwald didn't join our home to replace the enormous presences of those we lost; he joined it to honor the space they created. His life reminds me daily that the lessons we learned about prioritizing **dignity, comfort, and proactive planning** are not just for the end of life, they are the blueprints for a truly compassionate life at *every* stage.

So let us end this book not with sorrow, but with the quiet strength that comes from being prepared. The commitment made in these pages extends beyond the final decision: it is a perpetual vow to be their fierce advocate.

My hope is that through this shared experience, you feel empowered, informed, and—most importantly—**not alone** in navigating the weight of this most sacred responsibility. Keep seeking your village, keep advocating for higher standards, and keep honoring the unconditional love they give.

> *The love is not a thing to stop; it wraps around you,*
> *strong and vast. The broken piece you feel will drop,*
> *is just the empty space I've cast.*

Let us move forward, ensuring that every day we are given with our cherished companions is filled with meaning, comfort, and the absolute dignity they deserve.

— Angela Human

Acknowledgements

It takes a village to write a book, and this one is no exception. I want to express my deepest gratitude to everyone who contributed to its creation.

My Constant Companions

First and foremost, this book would not even exist without **Laurel**, my co-pet-parent and unwavering partner. Your endless patience, insightful feedback, and shared love for our furry companions were instrumental in bringing this book to life. Thank you for every late-night discussion, every shared laugh (and tear), and every moment of encouragement. You are my rock.

To **Zander, Murphy & Ozwald** (our current *furry mortals*). The love you give can never be measured. My hope is that we do right by you when the time comes to say goodbye and may that day be **VERY** far off.

The Storytellers

To all my family and friends who so generously shared their stories, thank you. Your willingness to open up about your experiences, triumphs, and heart-wrenching challenges provided the rich tapestry of anecdotes that truly make this book a living document. Each narrative added a unique layer of depth, humor, and heart, reminding us that while our journeys are individual, the language of the human-animal bond is universal. I am incredibly grateful for your trust and openness; by sharing your most vulnerable moments, you have created a sanctuary for other readers to find their own experiences reflected and validated. These stories are the heartbeat of these pages, turning abstract advice into a shared road map for loving and losing with grace.

The Foster Parents & Rescue Organizations

There are no words to express my gratitude to all of you for keeping our little guys safe until they could find their way to us. If you are looking for your next furry mortal, they might be just around the corner.

- Tootie & Liz - **Galveston Island Humane Society**
- Lucy - She found us.
- Zoey & Zack - **Citizens for Animal Protection** (went to get pet food at PetSmart and each came home with us ... those adoption days are dangerous!)
- Oliver - **Blue Heron Farm** - Lisa & Christian Seger - best foster parents EVER!
- Murphy – **Standish Humane Society** – she chose us.
- Zander - **Texas Animal Society** - BHF fostered his sister and we saw Zander (formerly Breez) on their Instagram account @blueherontexas.
- Ozwald - Our neighbor, Derek ... thank you for bringing home an abandoned litter of puppies for us to run into on our daily walk.

Beyond the Pages

Finally, to my broader **family and friends** who offered their support, understanding, and occasional much-needed distractions throughout this journey, thank you. Your belief in this project, and in me, kept me going through thick and thin.

Thank you all for being a part of this adventure.

Furry Mortal Resources

This list is a curated collection of resources that are dedicated to supporting pet parents and veterinary professionals in navigating the complex and often emotional landscape of end-of-life care for beloved companion animals.

The sources are organized into functional categories, providing a comprehensive view of the services, information, and support available.

This is an essential reference guide comprising various organizations, professional associations, specialized service providers, and informational platforms related to pet hospice, quality-of-life assessment, euthanasia, and grief support.

These sources were carefully researched and used in the making of this book to ensure the content is grounded in best practices, informed by veterinary expertise, and sensitive to the emotional needs of pet parents facing the final chapter with their furry family members.

Primary Inspiration

- *Being Mortal: Medicine and What Matters in the End* by **Atul Gawande:** A significant inspiration for the book's philosophy on end-of-life care for pets.
  Website: https://atulgawande.com/book/being-mortal/

Veterinary Hospice and In-Home Euthanasia Providers

These organizations primarily offer specialized, in-person clinical services focused on comfort care and euthanasia.

- **AHELP:** AHELP is Animal Hospice, End of Life, and Palliative Care Project We prepare, guide, and empower pet parents through their animal companion's journey – during illness, end of life, and beyond – to make compassionate decisions that promote quality of life on the path to the Rainbow Bridge.
  Website: https://www.ahelpproject.org/
- **BluePearl Pet Hospital:** Offers information on pet hospice and senior care, including in-home hospice services and virtual quality of life consultations.
  Website: https://bluepearlvet.com/
- **Caring Pathways:** Provides a quality-of-life scale (The HHHHHMM Scale) and other resources, along with veterinary services.
  Website: https://caringpathways.com/
- **CodaPet:** Making in-home pet euthanasia known and accessible across the United States.
  Website: https://www.codapet.com/
- **Honor Pet:** A company offering specialized, serene, and compassionate environments for pet euthanasia, often as an alternative to a traditional veterinary clinic setting.
  Website: https://www.honor.pet
- **Integrative Veterinary Services – Holistic Veterinary:** Holistic-based practice offering a range of alternative modalities like acupuncture, herbal therapy, and nutritional counseling.
  Website: https://integrativeveterinaryservices.com/
- **Journeys Home Pet Euthanasia:** Noted for its "Journeys Quality of Life Scale for Pets" and in-home services.
  Website: https://journeyspet.com/

- **Lap of Love:** A well-known organization specializing in veterinary hospice and in-home euthanasia, providing a quality-of-life scale.
  Website: https://www.lapoflove.com
- **VCA Animal Hospitals:** Offers information on comfort care, quality of life, and grief/bereavement resources through their hospital network.
  Website: https://vcahospitals.com/

Pet Loss Support and Grief Resources

These resources focus on the emotional and psychological aspects of grieving a pet.

- **Association for Pet Loss and Bereavement (APLB):** APLB's mission is to promote and expand the field of pet loss and grief support by providing pet family support services and resources that honor the human/animal bond.
  Website: https://www.aplb.org/
- **Center for Pet Loss Grief:** Provides one-on-one and online support to help individuals navigate the complex emotions associated with grieving the loss of a beloved pet.
  Website: https://centerforpetlossgrief.com
- **Psychology Today:** Features expert interviews and articles, including a blog post on pet hospice and natural death.
  Website: https://www.psychologytoday.com/us/blog/pets-and-their-people
- **The Parted Paw:** The Parted Paw is a compassionate and certified support service offering resources and guidance for pet loss, pet care professionals, and pet parents.
  Website: https://www.thepartedpaw.com/
- **The Ralph Site:** A resource dedicated to pet loss support, offering tips on how to cope when caring for a terminally ill pet.
  Website: https://www.theralphsite.com/

- **saudade paws:** saudade paws provides gentle, compassionate guidance and resources for pet caregivers and pet service professionals navigating a pet's final stage and the bereavement that follows.
  Website: https://saudadepaws.com/

Professional and Educational Veterinary Organizations

These groups set standards, provide guidelines, and offer specialized education for veterinary professionals and pet parents.

- **The American Animal Hospital Association (AAHA):** Provides a variety of guidelines and resources for pet parents and veterinarians, including senior care and end-of-life care guidelines.
  Website: https://www.aaha.org/
- **American Veterinary Medical Association (AVMA):** Provides valuable resources for pet parents and professionals on end-of-life care and euthanasia.
  Website: https://www.avma.org/
- **BrightHaven:** An organization focused on animal hospice, particularly on pain and comfort care.
  Website: https://www.brighthaven.org/
- **Chi University:** A source for specialized education in Traditional Chinese Veterinary Medicine (TCVM) for veterinary professionals.
  Website: https://chiu.edu/
- **DVM360:** A site for veterinary professionals, offering articles on topics like anticipatory grief and advancements in end-of-life care.
  Website: https://www.dvm360.com/

- **International Association for Animal Hospice and Comfort Care (IAAHPC):** A leading resource for professionals and pet parents seeking guidance on animal hospice and comfort care, offering certifications and searchable provider lists.
  Website: https://iaahpc.org/
- **Veterinary Partner - VIN:** A reliable resource from the Veterinary Information Network with articles on hospice, comfort care, and assessing quality of life.
  Website: https://veterinarypartner.vin.com/

Quality of Life Assessment & Planning Tools

These resources were used to create the **Furry Mortals QOL Assessment Tool**. They offer additional tools or technology to help pet parents plan or assess their pet's health status.

- **CodaPet:** An online resource that offers a quality-of-life questionnaire to help pet parents make difficult end-of-life decisions.
  Website: https://www.codapet.com/
- **EverAfter:** An end-of-life planning app that helps ensure peace of mind for loved ones, including furry mortals.
  Website: https://www.everafterapp.com/
- **Lap of Love:** Pet quality of life scale.
  Website: https://www.lapoflove.com/how-will-i-know-it-is-time/lap-of-love-quality-of-life-scale.pdf
- **The Ohio State University Veterinary Medical Center:** Provides a quality-of-life assessment tool to help pet parents determine when it's time to say goodbye.
  Website: https://vmc.vet.osu.edu/sites/default/files/documents/how-will-i-know_rev_mar2024ms_0.pdf
- **SmartVet:** Pet Quality of Life Scale in Normal, IL
  Website: https://thesmartvet.com/pet-quality-of-life-scale-normal-il/

General Information

Comprehensive informational sites and influential literature.

- **PetMD:** A comprehensive resource for pet parents, providing guidance on a wide range of topics from natural pain relief for pets to coping with pet loss and understanding hospice care.
  Website: https://www.petmd.com/

Non-Profits and Specific Missions

Groups with a dedicated mission, such as research or specific care types.

- **Moose's March Inc.:** Moose's March is dedicated to the early detection of pet cancer, aiming for better outcomes and an extended quality of life. In short, we are "Marching for More Memories."
  Website: https://www.moosesmarch.com/

Memorialization and Eco-Friendly Options

These companies offer traditional and eco-friendly memorials, burials, or cremation services.

- **Better Place Forests:** Better Place Forests offers a sustainable and comforting way to honor beloved pets by allowing their ashes to be spread at the base of a Memorial Tree, either in a shared ceremony with human remains or during a private pet-only spreading, thus providing a shared and protected final resting place.
  Website: https://www.betterplaceforests.com/blog/pet-ashes-memorial-forest/

- **The Companions Rest Group:** Companions Rest Memorials designs and sells handcrafted, artisan pet urns and memorials—primarily ceramic and wooden—that function as beautiful, home-decor pieces to honor the memory of a beloved dog or cat companion.
  Website: https://companionsrestmemorials.com/
- **Cremation by Water Group:** Cremation by Water offers an eco-friendly alternative to flame cremation, known as aquamation (alkaline hydrolysis), for pet farewells.
  Website: https://www.cremation-by-water.com/
- **Parting Stone:** Parting Stone offers a service to transform a dog's cremated ashes into a collection of 5–40 clean, smooth, naturally varying "stones," providing an alternative to conventional ash for memorializing a pet.
  Website: https://partingstone.com/pages/pets-solidified-remains
- **Senfina:** Honor your dear pet's love by growing a beautiful green memorial with eco-friendly pet urns made of beeswax.
  Website: https://senfina.eco/

furry
mortals
THE OLIVER PROJECT

www.ingramcontent.com/pod-product-compliance
Lightning Source LLC
Chambersburg PA
CBHW011234120626
46549CB00009B/3271